SEEDS OF LIBERTY

BOBBY AKART

SEEDS OF LIBERTY

INTERNATIONAL BEST SELLING AUTHOR
BOBBY AKART

THANK YOU

Thank you for reading **SEEDS OF LIBERTY,** an historical guide to the Boston Brahmin series by Author Bobby Akart.
Join Bobby Akart's mailing list to learn about upcoming releases, deals, and appearances. Follow this link to:
BobbyAkart.com

PRAISE FOR BOBBY AKART AND THE
BOSTON BRAHMIN SERIES

"I have highly enjoyed Mr. Akart's literary works because his research is comprehensive and he has an eerie prescience of writing 'fiction' before it becomes reality."

"The level of research, attention to detail and the quality of all the small stories within his stories, good enough to be standalone books on their own, that really set him at the top."

"I like to consider Bobby Akart's work as 'factual fiction' they are so well researched and present scenarios likely to happen."

"Bobby Akart is one of the best authors to come

along in a long time, and he works his craft very well in his Boston Brahmin series."

"There are very few authors who consistently deliver novels that I simply have to finish within 48 hours of their release, but Bobby Akart is one of those authors."

"The suspense, the behind the scenes machinations of governments, the evil unleashed, the world on an uncharted path are all woven into another excellent story."

"Bobby Akart gives a masterclass in the blending of real history with an edge of your seat story."

SEEDS OF LIBERTY

by
Bobby Akart

OTHER WORKS BY AMAZON CHARTS TOP 25 AUTHOR BOBBY AKART

The California Dreamin' Duology
ARkStorm (a standalone, disaster thriller)
Fractured (a standalone, disaster thriller)

The Perfect Storm Series
Perfect Storm 1
Perfect Storm 2
Perfect Storm 3
Perfect Storm 4

Black Gold (a standalone, terrorism thriller)

The Nuclear Winter Series

First Strike
Armageddon
Whiteout
Devil Storm
Desolation

New Madrid (a standalone, disaster thriller)

Odessa (a Gunner Fox trilogy)
Odessa Reborn
Odessa Rising
Odessa Strikes

The Virus Hunters
Virus Hunters I
Virus Hunters II
Virus Hunters III

The Geostorm Series
The Shift
The Pulse
The Collapse
The Flood

The Tempest
The Pioneers

The Asteroid Series (A Gunner Fox trilogy)
Discovery
Diversion
Destruction

The Doomsday Series
Apocalypse
Haven
Anarchy
Minutemen
Civil War

The Yellowstone Series
Hellfire
Inferno
Fallout
Survival

The Lone Star Series
Axis of Evil
Beyond Borders

Lines in the Sand
Texas Strong
Fifth Column
Suicide Six

The Pandemic Series
Beginnings
The Innocents
Level 6
Quietus

The Blackout Series
36 Hours
Zero Hour
Turning Point
Shiloh Ranch
Hornet's Nest
Devil's Homecoming

The Boston Brahmin Series
The Loyal Nine
Cyber Attack
Martial Law
False Flag

The Mechanics
Choose Freedom
Patriot's Farewell (standalone novel)
Black Friday (standalone novel)
Seeds of Liberty (Companion Guide)

The Prepping for Tomorrow Series (non-fiction)
Cyber Warfare
EMP: Electromagnetic Pulse
Economic Collapse

Copyright Information

The author and publisher have provided this eBook to you for your personal use only. You may not make this eBook publicly available in any way.

Copyright infringement is against the law. If you believe the copy of this eBook you are reading infringes on the author's copyright, please notify the publisher through BobbyAkart@gmail.com

© 2023 Wisteria Hall Inc. All rights reserved. Except as permitted under the U.S. Copyright Act of 1976, no part of this book may be reproduced, distributed or transmitted in any form or by any means including, but not limited to electronic, mechanical, photocopying, recording, or otherwise, or stored in a database or retrieval system, without the express written permission of Crown Publishers Inc.

DEDICATIONS

With the love and support of my wife, Dani, together with the unconditional love of Bullie and Boom, the princesses of the palace, I'm able to tell you these stories. It would be impossible for me to write without them in my heart.

Freedom and security are precious gifts that we, as Americans, should never take for granted. I would like to thank the members of America's Armed Forces, past and present, for willingly making sacrifices each day to provide us that freedom and security. Also, a note of thanks to their families who endure countless sleepless nights as their loved ones are deployed around the world.

To the Founding Fathers, whose vision and

bravery built America. For what we have become, I apologize.

Choose Freedom!

ACKNOWLEDGEMENTS

Writing a book that is both informative and entertaining requires a tremendous team effort.

For their efforts in making the Nuclear Winter series a reality, I would like to thank Hristo Argirov Kovatliev for his incredible artistic talents in creating my cover art. He and Dani collaborate (and conspire) to create the most incredible book covers in the publishing business. A huge hug of appreciation goes out to Pauline Nolet, the *Professor*, for her editorial prowess and patience in correcting this writer's same tics after nearly seventy novels. Thank you, Drew Avera, a United States Navy veteran, who has brought his talented formatting skills from a writer's perspective to create multiple formats for reading my novels.

Finally, as always, a special thank you to my team of loyal friends and readers who've always supported my work and provided me valuable insight over the years.

Thank you!

Choose Freedom!

ABOUT THE AUTHOR, BOBBY AKART

Author Bobby Akart has been ranked by Amazon as #25 on the Amazon Charts list of most popular, bestselling authors. He has achieved recognition as the #1 bestselling Horror Author, #1 bestselling Science Fiction Author, #5 bestselling Action & Adventure Author, #7 bestselling Historical Fiction Author and #10 on Amazon's bestselling Thriller Author list.

Mr. Akart has delivered up-all-night thrillers to readers in 245 countries and territories worldwide. He has sold over one million books in all formats, which includes over forty international bestsellers, in nearly fifty fiction and nonfiction genres.

His novel *Yellowstone: Hellfire* reached the Top 25 on the Amazon bestsellers list and earned him multiple Kindle All-Star awards for most pages read in a month and most pages read as an author. The Yellowstone series vaulted him to the #25 bestselling author on Amazon Charts, and the #1 bestselling science fiction author.

Since its release in December 2020, his stand-alone novel, New Madrid Earthquake, has been ranked #1 on Amazon Charts in multiple countries as a natural disaster thriller.

Mr. Akart is a graduate of the University of Tennessee after pursuing a dual major in economics and political science. He went on to obtain his master's degree in business administration and his doctorate degree in law at Tennessee.

With over a million copies of his novels in print, Bobby Akart has provided his readers a diverse range of topics that are both informative and entertaining. His attention to detail and impeccable research has allowed him to capture the imagination of his readers through his fictional works and bring them valuable knowledge through his nonfiction books.

SIGN UP for Bobby Akart's mailing list to learn of special offers, view bonus content, and be the first to receive news about new releases.

Visit www.BobbyAkart.com for details.

ABOUT SEEDS OF LIBERTY & THE BOSTON BRAHMIN SERIES

I hope you find *Seeds of Liberty*, a #1 bestseller in multiple Amazon genre categories, to be both informative and entertaining. *Seeds of Liberty* is a companion nonfiction guide to *The Boston Brahmin* series, which provides both a sociological analysis and a complete historical perspective of America's quest for independence.

In this historical treatise, as you will see, America has a penchant for rebellion. While the dates associated with the War for Independence are well known, the battle for freedom began many years before with the early colonists.

And this is good old Boston,

The home of the bean and the cod,
Where the Lowells talk only to Cabots,
And the Cabots talk only to God.

The *Boston Brahmin* series is the international bestselling political thriller series published in 2015 with subsequent standalone thrillers. Works of fiction are frequently based on historical fact. In the case of book one of the series, *The Loyal Nine*, and the entire *Boston Brahmin* series, history repeats itself.

The series takes the reader on a journey based on historical fact—both in its character development and the events that take place during the timeline of the series. The *Boston Brahmin* series is about the societal and economic collapse of America. This type of collapse event is gradual and not sudden. The events portrayed in the series will rise to a crescendo, forcing the characters to decide—choose tyranny or freedom. They will be challenged physically and emotionally. As always, nothing is what it seems.

The Loyal Nine takes its name from nine patriotic Bostonians who chose freedom over the tyrannical rule of Great Britain. As the British exerted more control over the colonists, especially in the form of taxes, anger and resentment rose to a crescendo, resulting in the War for Independence.

As the country slowly descends into economic and social despair, America is one bad news story away from collapse. In *Cyber Attack*, book two of the *Boston Brahmin* series, the reader is taken through a very realistic scenario that would bring America to its knees.

Writing a series of this magnitude takes a considerable amount of time and research. It also asks the reader to become invested in the journey of the characters. Creating a book series about societal and economic collapse is a marathon, not a sprint. Read with us. Learn with us. Get involved in the backstory and details of the novels.

I encourage you to interact with me on social media. Links to my accounts are available on my website, www.BobbyAkart.com. I truly enjoy conversing with my readers—all of whom I consider friends.

I hope you enjoy this epic, history-rich thriller series that begins with *Seeds of Liberty*. Written in 2015, it's a storyline torn from today's headlines. The *Boston Brahmin* series presents a nation plunged into chaos by enemies foreign and domestic.

Only the Loyal Nine, a patriotic group of descendants of our Founding Fathers, can navigate the collapse and restore the American republic.

Choose Freedom!

EPIGRAPH

We hold these truths to be self-evident, that all men are created equal, that they are endowed by their Creator with certain inalienable Rights, that among these are Life, Liberty and the pursuit of Happiness.
~ Declaration of Independence, July 4, 1776

The secret of freedom lies in educating people, whereas the secret of tyranny is in keeping them ignorant.
~ Maximilien Robespierre, French Politician (1758 – 1794)

Those who cannot remember the past are condemned to repeat it.
 ~ George Santayana, philosopher and novelist

America will never be destroyed from the outside. If we falter and lose our freedoms, it will be because we destroyed ourselves.
 ~ Abraham Lincoln

The following five attributes marked Rome at its end: first, a mounting love of show and luxury; second, a widening gap between the very rich and the very poor; third, an obsession with sex; fourth, freakishness in the arts, masquerading as originality, and enthusiasms pretending to be creativity; fifth, an increased desire to live off the state.
 ~ Edward Gibbon (1737-1794) in his Decline and Fall of the Roman Empire

The real rulers, you'll never see.
   ∼ Anonymous

PART ONE

Our Passion for Freedom Runs Deep

The Seeds of Liberty were sown long before the first shot was fired at Lexington and Concord in Massachusetts to begin the Revolutionary War. The American Colonists wanted their freedom from Great Britain and their desire would not easily be squelched.

Arguably, the very founding of our nation by those who braved the trip across the Atlantic Ocean was religious freedom. Not only did the settlers face persecution in the nations they fled, but upon arrival, the heavy thumb of Great Britain was held on their chest.

Consider those early days. The Mayflower

Compact, was the first official governing document by the English settlers who traveled to the New World on the Mayflower. These Pilgrims planned on settling in Northern Virginia to join a much smaller group. However, a vastly different result occurred.

The early colonists expected to enjoy the benefit of the vast Atlantic Ocean as a buffer from their kings which made direct rule nearly impossible. As a result, the principles of self-determination and sovereignty became ingrained in the early American psyche.

Unlike the early Virginians, the passengers on the Mayflower had no charter or patent to settle their new colony because they'd landed at Plymouth Rock in Massachusetts. As the passengers became aware of the situation, they decided they were free to create settlements of their own choosing and thus ignored any agreements which were being negotiated back in England.

While still on board the ship, they entered into a contract, known as the Mayflower Compact, to encourage cooperation among the settlers "for the general good of the Colony unto which we promise all due submission and obedience."

A governor was chosen, and town meetings became the norm throughout New England. The religious Pilgrims made equality a practice in the community, and the churches became the primary meetinghouse throughout the Middle Colonies. History has recognized The Mayflower Compact as the seed of American democracy, and it is widely recognized as the world's first written constitution.

The important steps toward independence were already realized by the American colonists during these early colonial years. Because of the vast distance between America and Europe, self-rule and independence became commonplace. Events in the late seventeenth century and the early part of the eighteenth century made independence from Britain even more inevitable.

The Age of Enlightenment, in the late 1600's, focused Europeans on reason, analysis and individualism, rather than traditional lines of authority represented by the monarchs and the church. This change in philosophy filled the heads of educated colonists with thoughts of liberty and progress. The Great Awakening, a spiritual renewal in the late seventeenth century, ushered in new faiths, where equality between ministers and the congregation was the norm. American newspapers became increasingly independent and freethinking.

Soon, a tradition of ignoring English law and

customs regulations was firmly established by New England smugglers. The colonists became accustomed to rebellion, as the settlers from New York to South Carolina rose in demands of equality. Diverse peoples from all over Europe flocked to the British colonies with absolutely no loyalty to the British Crown, seeking the opportunity to make their own way.

The passengers of the Mayflower Compact never expected to be blown hundreds of miles off course, to land in a place where their existing patent from the King of England had no standing. But with the Mayflower Compact, they crafted a powerful agreement that established self-rule, their right to worship as they wished, and the rule of law.

In that simple act, an initial defiance of the king, they laid the foundation for a nation that would become a beacon of freedom.

And, this was just the beginning.

A lesser known but perhaps more important moment occurred in 1657. A new sect of believers had emerged in England in the 1650s--the Religious Society of Friends, often referred to as Quakers, in a mocking manner, for their belief that *people should tremble at the word of the Lord*. They were considered radicals and were persecuted, in some cases even executed. They sought safety in the New World.

One Quaker named Robert Hodgson began to preach to crowds in New Netherland (New York). He was ordered arrested and flogged. This set off a firestorm within the community forcing the local government to act.

Peter Stuyvesant, director general of New Netherland, subsequently forbade people from allowing Quakers into their towns or giving them shelter in their homes. When his dictates were challenged, he was said to have responded, "We derive our authority from God and the West India Company, not from the pleasure of a few ignorant subjects."

The citizens of New Netherland were outraged. In yet another act of defiance against British Rule, Tobias Feake, the sheriff of Vlissingen, New Netherland (today known as Flushing, New York), and the town clerk, Edward Clark, drafted a petition calling for acceptance of the beliefs of others and their right to accept Quakers into their towns and homes. They persuaded 28 of their fellow citizens to stand with them in signing the petition. It was only 1657 and the colonists were already flexing their muscles.

History smiled upon their efforts. The petition

they drafted, known as the Flushing Remonstrance, survived as one of the most beautiful and inspiring statements of the American spirit. The Remonstrance ended as follows:

The law of love, peace and liberty in the states extending to Jews, Turks and Egyptians, as they are considered sonnes of Adam, which is the glory of the outward state of Holland, soe love, peace and liberty, extending to all in Christ Jesus, condemns hatred, war and bondage. And because our Saviour sayeth it is impossible but that offences will come, but woe unto him by whom they cometh, our desire is not to offend one of his little ones, in whatsoever form, name or title hee appears in, whether Presbyterian, Independent, Baptist or Quaker, but shall be glad to see anything of God in any of them, desiring to doe unto all men as we desire all men should doe unto us, which is the true law both of Church and State; for our Saviour sayeth this is the law and the prophets.

Therefore if any of these said persons come in love unto us, we cannot in conscience lay violent hands upon them, but give them free egresse and regresse unto our Town, and houses, as God shall persuade our consciences, for we are bounde by the law of God and man to doe good unto all men and evil to noe man. And this is according to the patent and charter of our

Towne, given unto us in the name of the States General, which we are not willing to infringe, and violate, but shall houlde to our patent and shall remaine, your humble subjects, the inhabitants of Vlishing.

In rejecting the prohibition against receiving or entertaining Quakers, the signatories of the Flushing Remonstrance stated:

We desire therefore in this case not to judge least we be judged, neither to condemn least we be condemned, but rather let every man stand or fall to his own Master ...

Therefore if any of these said persons come in love unto us, we cannot in conscience lay violent hands upon them, but give them free egresse and regresse unto our Town, and houses, as God shall persuade our consciences, for we are bounde by the law of God and man to doe good unto all men and evil to noe man.

Naturally, the King could not let this stand. Feake and Clark paid a heavy price for this act of conscience as they were immediately imprisoned and fined. But their spirit of liberty and resistance prevailed. Eventually the Dutch West India Company had a change of heart and ordered Stuyvesant to *allow everyone to have his own belief.*

It was a little over 100 years later when the right

to freedom of belief was codified in the Bill of Rights. Many historians tend to think of Thomas Jefferson as the father of our freedoms for having inspired the Bill of Rights, or James Madison for having drafted them, but the Seeds of Liberty were paved by ordinary citizens, such as the thirty who signed the Flushing Remonstrance.

Meanwhile, near the turn of the seventeenth century, The Virginia House of Burgesses became the first representative assembly in the Western Hemisphere. Established by the Virginia Company, a business charter created for the purposes of building settlements in North America, the House of Burgesses not only created stability in the Virginia colony, but it was used to encourage entrepreneurs from Europe to settle the new land. The Burgesses formulated their own rules and regulations to govern Virginia, while abandoning those suggested by their namesake, Elizabeth I — The Virgin Queen.

Yet another act of defiance as more Seeds of Liberty are sown.

Famed British statesman and former Prime Minister of the United Kingdom, Winston Churchill once said, "The future is unknowable, but the past should give us hope."

The lessons learned from the that small band of

thirty citizens in Flushing, New York, should serve to remind ourselves that the American commitment to liberty does not depend on singular individuals such as Madison or Jefferson, or on a president or governor, but it depends fully on the love for liberty each one of us holds and the lengths we are willing to go to uphold it.

PART TWO

From Defiance to Revolutionary Thinking

Revolutions tend to be brutal affairs. The French Revolution in the late eighteenth century was a period of radical social and political upheaval in European history, culminating in the rise to power of Napoleon, a ruthless emperor who tried to conquer Europe. The Great October Socialist Revolution, a part of the Bolshevik Revolution of 1917, brought years of civil war and systematic genocide by Joseph Stalin. The Russian people likely yearned for a return to the days of their Tsarist autocratic rulers after a decade or so of that "revolution." The Chinese Cultural Revolution of the early twentieth century was a series of great political upheavals, which overthrew the imperial Manchu dynasty. Communist rule was established under the leadership of Mao Zedong, sentencing uncounted millions to death. More recently, revolutions in Cuba and Iran resulted in similar, tyrannical regimes.

How did the American Revolution yield a constitutional republic, with greater freedom on a large scale than the world had ever seen?

Successful revolutions never begin overnight. The American Revolution was two centuries in the making. Beginning with the early attempts at English colonization on Roanoke Island in 1585, and throughout the early settling of the new world, important stones were laid into the foundation of American freedom and independence.

Revolutions were generally born when the social climate in a country change or a crisis besets a nation, whether brought about by fiscal mismanagement, war, or a failure of government. Consider this modern example.

On December 17, 2010, a Tunisian street vendor named Mohamed Bouazizi set himself on fire after the police confiscated his fruit stand.

His death struck a chord with young people around the country and throughout the Middle East. Within days, protests erupted around the region, from Syria to Egypt and Libya, as millions demanded economic, political, and social reforms from governments that were stubbornly and habitually unresponsive to their ultimatums. These acts of civil disobedience had been extremely rare in these countries, where authoritarian leaders forbade political dissent.

However, despite taking place at the same time and in neighboring countries, these revolutions—known as the *Arab Spring*—yielded dramatically different outcomes. Tunisia successfully ousted its longtime dictator and transitioned to a democracy. Libya, Syria, and Yemen descended into devastating civil wars that continued for a decade. In Egypt, citizens voted in the country's first free and fair election in 2012, only for a counterrevolution the following year to install yet another military regime.

Some revolutions begin suddenly, taking rulers by surprise, ousting a regime, and resulting in dramatic political change. Others go on for years and end with the government and revolutionaries at the negotiating table, perhaps agreeing to reforms such as a power-sharing agreement. Still others are stopped short, with the government resuming control —often after brutal crackdowns.

One might ask, why are some movements

successful in overthrowing their government while others fail to do so?

In today's digital world, governments are able to restrict, monitor, and censor social media, which prevents demonstrators from gathering and helps rulers target political activists and deflate protest movements.

In Iran, for example, the government shut down the internet for a week amid countrywide protests in 2019, which made organizing demonstrations more difficult and hampered news reporting on the situation.

Even in the United States, government officials, law enforcement, and political leaders pressured media, both social and news, to restrict or even block the content during Pandemic years of 2020-21.

In certain instances, governments attempt to crush protest movements with forceful crackdowns. Egyptian security forces, for example, killed hundreds of their fellow citizens during a 2013 demonstration that challenged the country's new military regime. But what happens if the military refuses to fire on protesters and instead stands in solidarity with revolutionaries? In such instances, the government is left largely powerless, as was the case when the Tunisian military supported the country's Arab Spring protest movement.

Successful movements need to agree on aims. Anyone who has worked on a group project in a school setting, or at work, knows how difficult it is to manage expectations, the workload, and the final outcome. When revolutionaries can't agree on goals and how to accomplish them, they risk splintering into a patchwork of movements, often with competing agendas.

This was the case in Syria, where scores of different rebel groups took up arms against the country's government but could not agree on what a political settlement should look like. It might've been the case in America had it not been for a small group of influential colonists, the Loyal Nine, who were able to bring the competing factions together, for the most part.

Sometimes, acts of defiance yield results in a short period of time. In the case of American history, it took nearly two hundred years.

PART THREE

America's Penchant for Rebellion

The American colonies had known violent rebellion long before the Revolutionary War. Each of the original thirteen colonies had experienced violent uprisings. Americans had shown themselves more than willing to take up arms to defend a cause held dear. This tradition of rebellion characterized the American spirit throughout its early history.

King Philip's War (1675)

Considered the first major Indian war in the new

world, it is also known as the bloodiest war in American history on a per capita basis. At the center of the conflict was one man, Metacom. He was the leader of the Pkanokets Indian tribe, which resided in Massachusetts, Connecticut, Rhode Island and Maine. The son of Massasoit, the beloved chief who helped the Pilgrims survive their first winter, Metacom adopted the name King Phillip to pay homage to his father. After the Pilgrims arrival in 1620, the new colonist's prospered, multiplied and expanded their settlements throughout New England. In the meantime, the Indians experienced a slow state of decline from diseases introduced by the Europeans, in addition to the loss of tribal lands. King Philip stepped forward to make a stand, setting the stage for a conflict with the settlers. He infamously stated, "I am determined not to live until I have no country".

As is often case, war broke out over the simplest of disagreements. English cattle often broke through their fences and trampled Indian corn. In one instance, several Wampanoag braves retaliated by killing colonist owned cattle. Shortly later, a farmer retaliated by killing an Indian, igniting the powder keg known as King Philip's War. After four long, bloody years, Metacom was killed, and the war came to an end.

King Philip's War is historically significant because the trials and tribulations of the colonists were handled without significant English government support. America as a whole created an identity separate and distinct from of subjects of the king. This did not go unnoticed by the British royal government. England tried to gain control over the colonies, but they lost control of the American psyche.

Bacon's Rebellion (1676)

One of the earliest large-scale insurrections was Bacon's Rebellion. In Virginia, the administration of Governor Sir William Berkeley became unpopular with farmers and settlers for a number of reasons. Governor Berkeley instituted a land ownership requirement to grant a citizen the right to vote. Taxes were raised to help pay for governmental activities yet protection from Indian attacks was lacking.

Exactly one hundred years before the Declaration of Independence, America saw its first armed rebellion against colonial rule. In 1676, a social climbing young official named Nathaniel Bacon led an army of one-thousand Virginia colonists against the governor, William Berkeley.

The 29-year-old militia leader and his followers were fed up with Berkeley's puzzling lack of zeal in pursuing Indian war parties that had been massacring settlers along the colony's frontier. Many suspected that the governor's own personal involvement in the fur trade made him reluctant to retaliate against tribes that supplied his business partners with valuable pelts.

In one instance, Bacon and his men stormed the legislature and levelled their muskets at the colonial assembly including the governor himself and threatened to fire if the officials didn't authorize reprisals against the Indians. Berkeley relented and signed.

After issuing declaration against the colony's leadership, Bacon and his small army waged a bloody guerrilla campaign against local native populations (many of which actually had little to do with the contentious raids). He then marched on Jamestown and burned the capital to the ground.

Bacon, a distant relative of Governor Berkeley, met with a group of disgruntled citizens from the western part of Virginia eastward. They agree to join in a search of justice because they felt their interests were not represented by Virginia's colonial legislature. In the minds of the rural settlers, Governor Berkeley had done nothing to protect them from Indian raids. These frontier Virginians claimed Berkeley failed to incorporate their businesses into the lucrative eastern seaboard marketplaces.

Bacon raised a small army. In September of 1676, over a thousand of Bacon's followers entered Jamestown and burned the capital city. Governor Berkeley fled until reinforcements could organize. The rebels pillaged and plundered the countryside until Berkeley's forces crushed them. Over twenty rebels were hanged, but fear of further rebellion was struck into the hearts of the members of the wealthy Virginia planting class.

Soon, reinforcements from England streamed into the colony and drove the rebel army into hiding. Bacon himself succumbed to dysentery later that fall. At least 23 of the rebels were arrested and hanged and the uprising collapsed. Despite being a personal friend of King Charles II, Berkeley himself was recalled for his poor handling of the entire affair. His successor won favor among colonists by lowering taxes and cracking down on native tribes.

Bacon's rebellion resulted in the ouster of Governor Berkeley. Progress was made in thwarting Indian attacks resulting in a peace treaty and the frontiersman gained a foothold for their goods in eastern Virginia.

Culpeper's Rebellion (1677)

Similar uprisings took place all along the colonial backwoods. Culpeper's Rebellion took place in 1677 through 1678. The rebellion came in response to a variety of complaints about the government but arose as a reaction to the Navigation Acts imposed upon the colonies starting in 1651.

In order to control the benefits of trade generated by the colonists, British rule prohibited the colonies from trading directly with Spain, France and the Netherlands. These trade controls gave rise to extensive smuggling and increased angst between the early settlers and England. Culpeper's Rebellion was the result of an escalation of these hostilities. Despite attempts by Governor Peter Carteret to convince England to abandon the Navigation Acts, the law was strengthened — as was its enforcement.

The regulations, which prohibited the colonies from trading with any other power except England, also levied onerous tariffs on exports from the Americas bound for the British Isles. Business interests within the colony opposed the law and took action against its enforcers.

The rebels moved swiftly and overthrew the governor, Thomas Miller. They next established their own government and appointed John Culpeper, a member of the South Carolina parliament and its surveyor general, governor. Miller escaped the usurpers and made for England to report the insurrection. Culpepper pursued Miller to London and personally presented his grievances to the directors of the colony, known as the Lords Proprietors of Carolina.

Amazingly, some of the controlling interests expressed sympathy for the rebels and set Culpepper free. One of the wealthiest of the rebel ringleaders, George Durant, was named interim governor. He immediately pardoned his compatriots and order was restored.

Finally, the freedom loving colonists had enough. Culpepper gathered up some armed supporters and they stormed the home of British loyalists who enforced the Navigation Act. Their ranks swelled and soon colonists loyal to Culpeper seized the reins of government in the Carolinas. The colonists enjoyed peace and the government ran more smoothly under self-rule.

The Rebellions of 1689

In 1688, England's Catholic monarch, James II, was toppled by the Dutch protestant William of Orange. And it wasn't long before the ensuing sectarian strife, known as the Glorious Revolution, spread to the colonies. In fact, the troubles prompted at least two violent uprisings in the New World the following year.

Upon learning in April of 1689 that the English throne had changed hands, residents of the Massachusetts colony, known at the time as the Dominion of New England, removed the widely unpopular and draconian governor Sir Edmund Andros along with several of his officials. It was more than just Andros' heavy-handed rule that colonists had grown to despise – local Puritans disapproved of the 52-year-old Londoners' Anglican pedigree. The rebels held Andros in a fort in Boston Harbor and even seized the captain of one of the King's warships, HMS Rose.

Eventually the new regime in London recalled Andros, much to the delight of crowds in Boston. However, a number of the uprisings' ringleaders were taken to England in chains. Meanwhile in nearby New York colony, a 49-year-old German-born Calvinist and militia captain named Jacob Leisler commanded an insurrection that chased Governor Francis Nicholson from office.

The predominantly Dutch rebels were emboldened by the coronation of William of Orange of the Netherlands to the English throne and used the occasion to remove the hated colonial elites. But with yet another war against France in the offing, Leisler appointed himself governor of New York and sent troops up the Hudson River Valley to protect the colony from French and Indian invaders. He even organized an ill-fated invasion of Quebec in 1690. In the spring of 1691, an army of English regulars arrived in New York and demanded Leisler surrender. He was hanged for treason.

The Bloody Paxton Boys (1764)

The Paxton Boys uprising was less a rebellion as it was a massacre.

Following a series of bloody raids by Indians throughout the Lower Great Lakes and the Ohio Country, outraged settlers in Pennsylvania's frontier country demanded the colonial government in Philadelphia punish local tribes for the bloodshed. While the authorities vacillated, a force of several hundred farmers under the command of a firebrand reverend named John Elder exacted their revenge against the first aboriginals they could find.

On Dec. 14, 1763, Elder's men, who called themselves the Paxton Boys, attacked a village of Christianized Susquehannock natives at Conestoga Town and slaughtered the inhabitants. After scalping and mutilating the dead, the homesteaders then razed the village. Survivors of the attack, including women and children, sought refuge in nearby Lancaster.

The rebels tracked them there and murdered 14 more. Even as officials expressed outrage over the atrocities and offered huge bounties for the capture of any perpetrator, the Paxton Boys next marched on Philadelphia itself. They were intercepted by a delegation of civic leaders including Benjamin Franklin who convinced them to lay down their weapons and return home.

The Paxton Boys demonstrated the interrelationship between colonial violence and rhetoric although their actions were not directed at British rule, initially. They set the precedent for future violence by the Colonists in their quest for freedom by taking their independence into their own hands.

At Philadelphia, they were allowed to air their grievances. However, none were ever arrested.

The seeds of revolutionary thinking had taken root, and the stage was set for Americans to assert their independence from their British brothers and sisters. Many events transpired between the one-hundred-year period of 1676 and 1776 that served as precursors to the American Revolution. In many ways, the American Revolution had been completed before any of the actual fighting began. The roots had already grown.

PART FOUR

The Prelude to the Revolutionary War

The Boston Massacre (1770)

On this day, the Boston Massacre lit the fuse of revolution.

It was March 5, 1770, when British soldiers fired upon a group of rowdy colonists, killing five and wounding others. "On that night, the foundation of American Independence was laid," wrote John Adams. "Not the Battle of Lexington or Bunker Hill, not the surrender of Burgoyne or Cornwallis, were more important events in American history than the battle of King Street on the 5th of March, 1770."

In front of the Custom House on King Street in Boston, British soldiers fired upon a group of colonists, killing three instantly and two later as a result of their wounds. There were varying accounts of what happened, but most people agree that the soldiers were provoked by a group of rowdy colonists and that someone yelled "fire" – though no one knows who.

Before that night, tensions had been rising in Boston for some time. After the Stamp Act was repealed, Britain felt the need to show that it still had control over the colonies, so Parliament passed a series of acts known as the Townshend Acts. These laws were designed to tax the colonies on imports they could only get from Great Britain, such as glass, paper, and tea.

The British thought that since this was an external tax – unlike the Stamp Act, which was internal – the colonists would not object. This, of course, was not the case. In 1768, John Dickinson wrote a series of letters in which he outlined how many colonists wished not to be taxed purely for revenue for the British empire.

On March 5, 1770, the Bostonians were fuming over taxes and constant surveillance by the British military, both of which had started two years prior.

As a result, a small disagreement between a wigmaker apprentice and a soldier easily escalated to a small riot. Henry Knox, the future Secretary of War, was one of the first colonists on the scene, and told the soldier, Private Hugh White, that if he fired a shot, he would die.

Through the course of the day, a crowd of more than two hundred colonists came to the defense of the apprentice. White eventually felt unsafe enough to call for help. He sent a messenger to get Captain Thomas Preston and his battalion of seven troops as backup. Allegedly, the protestors became more violent, throwing objects at the soldiers and jeering at them. As the scene was becoming more and more chaotic, Preston did not make any orders, but someone yelled *fire* leading the soldiers to shoot into the crowd.

When the dust cleared, three colonists were dead, and two others died later as a result of their wounds. The first three were Crispus Attucks, Samuel Gray, and James Caldwell; the other two were Samuel Maverick and Patrick Carr. Historically, Attucks was considered the most famous African American of the Revolutionary War and eventually became a symbol for the abolitionist movement.

After the massacre, the soldiers were represented by future President John Adams and Josiah Quincy II. Adams and Quincey took up the defense in order to show the British that the colonies could conduct a fair trial. Most of the soldiers ended up being acquitted, including Thomas Preston, who was found innocent because he never ordered the shots. Two soldiers were found guilty of manslaughter, and their hands were branded with an "M" as their punishment.

The incident fueled the anger of colonists like Samuel Adams and Paul Revere. They used the massacre as propaganda, recreating a Henry Pelham painting and distributing copies all over the Boston area in order to incite the public.

Revere made every effort to cast the British in a more negative light. The biggest misrepresentation was the depiction of each side. The Bostonians looked scared and out of sorts, while the British looked as if they were carrying out a planned attack. Although accounts differ, there was agreement that the whole thing was a mess, and that in no way were the British organized.

The British ended up withdrawing their troops from Boston and positioning them on an island off the coast of Massachusetts. While the Revolutionary

War would not start for another six years, this first bloody encounter attracted more attention to patriot groups like the Sons of Liberty and the Loyal Nine who would set the war in motion.

The War of the Regulation (1771)

Considered by some to be a prelude to Revolutionary War, the so-called War of the Regulation was a violent insurrection by settlers in the North Carolina backcountry against crooked tax collectors and sheriffs.

Throughout the 1760s, officials operating in the interior of the colony bullied farmers into handing over as much as twice the required levy only to then pocket the difference. To make matters worse, the colony's governor, William Tryon, was aware his administrators were on the take but turned a blind eye to their corruption. After years of abuse, thousands of disgruntled settlers banded together to drive off the tax collectors by force and establish their own local government.

The group called themselves *The Regulators*.

Their spokesperson was a 47-year-old Quaker preacher turned legislator named Herman Husband. Despite his pacifist upbringing, Husband accompanied more than 2,000 armed rebels against a battalion of several hundred colonial troops. Governor Tryon himself led the campaign to crush the uprising.

On May 19, 1771, the two armies met at Alamance. Husband hoped to avoid bloodshed. As the governor's troops advanced, the clergyman fled leaving the disorganized formation to the mercy of the advancing soldiers. Nearly forty North Carolinians died in the ensuing battle. The ill-equipped Regulators were utterly routed in minutes and seven accused ringleaders were captured and subsequently hanged. Husband escaped, making his way to Maryland. Tryon was appointed governor of New York.

The Boston Tea Party (1773)

The French and Indian War kept the British busy from 1754 to 1763. During this time, the unruly colonists defied British rule at every opportunity.

Victory in the war was costly for the British. At the war's conclusion in 1763, King George III and his government looked to taxing the American colonies as a way of recouping their war costs. They were also looking for ways to reestablish control over the colonial governments that had become increasingly independent while the Crown was distracted by the war. Royal ineptitude compounded the problem.

A series of actions including the Stamp Act (1765), the Townsend Acts (1767) and the Boston Massacre (1770) agitated the colonists, straining relations with the mother country. But it was the Crown's attempt to tax tea that spurred the colonists to action and laid the groundwork for the American Revolution.

The colonies refused to pay the levies required by the Townsend Acts claiming they had no obligation to pay taxes imposed by a Parliament in which they had no representation. In response, Parliament retracted the taxes with the exception of a duty on tea - a demonstration of Parliament's ability and right to tax the colonies.

In May of 1773 Parliament concocted a clever plan. They gave the struggling East India Company a monopoly on the importation of tea to America. Additionally, Parliament reduced the duty the colonies would have to pay for the imported tea. The

Americans would now get their tea at a cheaper price than ever before.

However, if the colonies paid the duty tax on the imported tea, they would be acknowledging Parliament's right to tax them. Tea was a staple of colonial life - it was assumed that the colonists would rather pay the tax than deny themselves the pleasure of a cup of tea.

The colonists were not fooled by Parliament's ploy. When the East India Company sent shipments of tea to Philadelphia and New York the ships were not allowed to land. In Charleston the tea-laden ships were permitted to dock but their cargo was consigned to a warehouse where it remained for three years until it was sold by patriots in order to help finance the revolution.

In Boston, the arrival of three tea ships ignited a furious reaction. The crisis came to a head on December 16, 1773, when as many as seven-thousand agitated locals milled about the wharf where the ships were docked. A mass meeting at the Old South Meeting House led by the Loyal Nine that morning resolved that the tea ships should leave the harbor without payment of any duty.

A committee was selected to take this message to the Customs House to force release of the ships out of the harbor. The Collector of Customs refused to allow the ships to leave without payment of the duty.

Stalemate.

The committee reported back to the mass meeting and a howl erupted from the meeting hall. It was now early evening and a group of about 200 men, some disguised as Indians, assembled on a nearby hill. Whooping war chants, the crowd marched two-by-two to the wharf, descended upon the three ships and dumped their offending cargos of tea into the harbor waters.

George Hewes, one of the Loyal Nine, was a member of the band of "Indians" that boarded the tea ships that evening. His recollection of the event was published some years later. Here is a portion of the story as the group makes its way to the tea-laden ships:

"It was now evening, and I immediately dressed myself in the costume of an Indian, equipped with a small hatchet, which I and my associates denominated the tomahawk, with which, and a club, after having painted my face and hands with coal dust in the shop of a blacksmith, I repaired to Griffin's wharf, where the ships lay that contained the tea. When I first appeared in the street after being thus disguised, I fell in with many who were dressed, equipped and

painted as I was, and who fell in with me and marched in order to the place of our destination.

"*When we arrived at the wharf, there were three of our number who assumed an authority to direct our operations, to which we readily submitted. They divided us into three parties, for the purpose of boarding the three ships which contained the tea at the same time. The name of him who commanded the division to which I was assigned was Leonard Pitt. The names of the other commanders I never knew.*

"*We were immediately ordered by the respective commanders to board all the ships at the same time, which we promptly obeyed. The commander of the division to which I belonged, as soon as we were on board the ship, appointed me boatswain, and ordered me to go to the captain and demand of him the keys to the hatches and a dozen candles. I made the demand accordingly, and the captain promptly replied, and delivered the articles; but requested me at the same time to do no damage to the ship or rigging. We then were ordered by our commander to open the hatches and take out all the chests of tea and throw them overboard, and we immediately proceeded to execute his orders, first cutting and splitting the chests with our tomahawks, so as thoroughly to expose them to the effects of the water.*

"In about three hours from the time we went on board, we had thus broken and thrown overboard every tea chest to be found in the ship, while those in the other ships were disposing of the tea in the same way, at the same time. We were surrounded by British armed ships, but no attempt was made to resist us.

"...The next morning, after we had cleared the ships of the tea, it was discovered that very considerable quantities of it were floating upon the surface of the water; and to prevent the possibility of any of its being saved for use, a number of small boats were manned by sailors and citizens, who rowed them into those parts of the harbor wherever the tea was visible, and by beating it with oars and paddles so thoroughly drenched it as to render its entire destruction inevitable."

Most colonists applauded the action while the reaction in London was swift and vehement. In March 1774 Parliament passed the Intolerable Acts which among other measures closed the Port of Boston.

The fuse that led directly to the explosion of American independence was lit.

The Intolerable Acts (1774)

The Intolerable Acts as dubbed by the Colonists was actually known as Coercive Acts, the titles referring to the laws that the British Parliament passed in 1774. These laws were very much a part of the ongoing uprising of what was the American Revolution.

Primarily in response to the Boston Tea Party, the British Parliament used Massachusetts as an example to turn around the trend of colonial resistance to the parliament that had had begun years prior. Four of the Acts dealt with the aftermath of the Boston Tea Party. The fifth, The Quebec Act, widened the boundaries of what was the province of Quebec and made changes that were in favor to the region's inhabitants that were French Catholic.

The Seven Years' War put a dent on the relationship between the Kingdom of Great Britain and Thirteen Colonies in 1763. The war put British government in great debt, and in the effect to increase revenues, the British Parliament increased the revenues of its taxes from the colonies. The Parliament believed that it was backed up by the Stamp Act of 1765 and the Townshend Act of 1767. This was in terms of legitimacy of letting the colonists pay more taxes to the British Empire. In effect, the Stamp Act and the Townshend Act were repealed while the Parliament according to Declaratory Act of 1766 stood its ground in upholding their rights to legislate the colonies in all cases.

According to the British Constitution, one cannot take away the property or taxes of a British subject without representation in the Parliament. However, since the colonies were not represented in the Parliament, the colonies fought against the Parliaments' devious acts, with some even saying the Parliament has no right to take away and use the taxes. This they clearly expressed in the slogan: *No taxation without representation.*

Colonial essays went further after the Townshend Act by questioning the legitimacy of the Parliament's jurisdiction in the colonies. The American Revolution was all about the true nature of the Parliament's Sovereignty.

The Colonists organized the Boston Tea Party for having been taxed by the Parliament without their consent. After England learned about this act of rebellion in January 1774, the British government's punished Boston with a series of acts for allegedly destroying privates. The acts were also meant to put back British Authority in Massachusetts and eventually reform the colonies in America.

It was in April 1774 that Prime Minister Lord North presented his defense of these acts to the House Commons. He pointed out how the Americans have disobeyed the laws of authority. In the face of risk, the Prime Minister, admonished the audience that something should be done otherwise all is lost.

Throughout the Colonies, outrage erupted. Richard Henry Lee of Virginia described the Acts as being, "a most wicked System for destroying the liberty of America."

The Acts, provided, in part:

1. The Boston Port Act, in direct response to the Boston Tea Party, initiated the closure of the Boston port until the repayment of the East India Company of destroyed tea and until order was restored to the King's satisfaction. This irked the Colonists as all of Boston was punished for individual acts and the punishment came without any due process in the courts at all.

2. The Massachusetts Government Act earned more ire than the Port Act because it changed the Massachusetts' government unilaterally so the British government would have full control. The second modified the Massachusetts Charter of 1691, taking away many of its rights of self-government. It was aimed at punishing Boston and forcing it out of

resistance. Almost all positions in the colonial government were to be appointment by the governor or directly by the King. Activities of town meetings were limited. Massachusetts was very proud of its independence and was angry at this infringement on its rights.

3. The Administration of Justice Act enabled the transfer of accused royal officials to another colony or even England. This measure would require witnesses to travel, the practical effect of which was thought to be that the British officials would escape justice. Although the act provided that travel expenses will be shouldered by the government, it was believed to be unnecessary because it was just an opportunity for the British to harass Americans and run from the law. George Washington even said that it was the "Murder Act" because it opened doors for harassment for the British. On their end, other colonies also believed that justice was served fairly to the British soldiers and pointed to the Boston Massacre in 1770 as an example.

4. The Quartering Act was the kind of act that covered all colonies and aimed to make a better housing program for the British troops in America. While in the previous acts the colonies were the ones that provided housing for the soldiers. If the local

legislatures were not cooperative, the fourth measure allowed the British to quarter British soldiers in colonial buildings at the expense of the colonists, including colonists' homes, if there was insufficient space in other buildings.

5. The Quebec Act was a legislation that was marginally related to the Coercive Acts because it did not have anything to do with Boston. The fifth act extended the boundaries of the province of Quebec. Because Quebec did not have representative assemblies, many colonists thought this transfer of land from the colonies to unrepresented Quebec was another attempt to punish the colonies and solidify British control.

However, the Quebec Act denied the people an elected legislative assembly. The oath of allegiance was also free of references to both the Protestant and Catholic faith. This naturally caused offense in the British colonies. Objections by the land speculators and settlers were mostly about transfer of lands. Some Colonists were afraid of the status of Catholicism in Quebec as there was a movement by the French Canadians to punish British Americans.

PART FIVE

The Loyal Nine (1764 – 1776)

George Grenville was a British statesman born into an influential political family. He became the British Prime Minister in 1763, and the primary focus of his government was to bring spending under control. Grenville, a Whig, advocated the supremacy of Parliament and a strong central government.

During his term in office from 1763 to 1765, a major point of contention at the time was the incredible cost of defending and protecting the colonies and the British expansion into the American frontier. Near the Appalachian Mountains, the British had stationed ten thousand troops for this purpose. While serving as Prime Minister of Great Britain in

1764, he proposed a stamp tax in a speech to Parliament. The new tax was imposed on all American colonists and required them to pay a tax on every piece of printed paper they used. Documents, licenses, newspapers, ship's papers, legal documents, and even playing cards were taxed. The money collected by the Stamp Act was to be used to help pay the costs of garrisoning the troops.

On February 17, 1765, the Stamp Act was passed in the House of Commons by an overwhelming vote of 205 to 49; on March 8, it unanimously passed in the House of Lords; and on March 22, it was given Royal Assent. The law had an effective date of November 1, 1765.

News of the Stamp Act's passage reached America in May of 1765. The Stamp Act caused both anger and resentment in the colonies—not so much because of the imposition of a tax, but because of its manner of enactment and means of enforcement. The colonists believed that it violated their rights as Englishmen to be taxed without their consent. Such consent, in the view of the colonists, could only be granted by the legislatures of the colonies in which they resided. The colonists believed that any laws passed affecting them were illegal under the British Bill of Rights of 1689.

A slogan was quickly adopted throughout the colonies: *No taxation without representation.*

Boston, Massachusetts, became the epicenter of the colonist opposition to British rule. In 1765 a group of Bostonians formed a "social club"—attempting to avoid the scrutiny a political organization might provoke. Their purpose, however, was more than social. This group of nine Bostonians, formed and operating in secrecy, plotted a response to the Stamp Act.

They called themselves the *Loyal Nine*. Although they were respectable merchants and tradesmen, they were not necessarily the most prominent Bostonians. They were private and unassuming, avoided undue publicity, and were diligent in their secretiveness. The names of the Loyal Nine aren't prominent in American history books. But these nine men sowed the seeds of the American Revolution. They were average, hardworking Americans—fighting against tyrannical rule.

They were:

Henry Bass, a merchant and the cousin of Samuel Adams; Thomas Chase, a distiller; John Avery, also a distiller and the Loyal Nine's secretary; Stephen Cleverly and John Smith, braziers (tradesmen who worked with brass); Thomas Crafts, a painter; Joseph Field, a seafarer; George Trott, a jeweler; and the most well-known among the Loyal Nine, Benjamin Edes, the printer of the *Boston Gazette*.

John Adams recalled in his diary that the Loyal Nine met in one of two locations; *either in a small compting Room in Chase and Speakman's Distillery or under the foliage of a large elm tree in nearby Hanover Square.* The tree would soon become known as the *Liberty Tree*. Until its destruction by British soldiers in 1775, the Liberty Tree would serve as a meeting place for fiery speeches and as a rallying point for patriotic demonstrations.

Knowing they were going to need help organizing a resistance movement, the Loyal Nine turned to Ebenezer Mackintosh and his gang of miscreants known as the South Enders. Mackintosh was a poor shoemaker who was generally considered lower class in Boston at the time. After the death of his first wife, Mackintosh became involved in the militia and later joined the infamous Fire Engine Company No. 9 in South Boston. Over time, he became a fixture and a leader in the poor communities of Boston's South End.

As the head of the fast-growing South End gang, he coordinated activities of the annual Guy Fawkes

Night held on the fifth of November. In 1605, Guy Fawkes was a member of the Gunpowder Plot to assassinate King James and several members of the House of Lords. The plot failed, but Fawkes became well known for his insurgent activities. Animated masks honoring Fawkes began to surface, featuring an oversized smile and red cheeks, a wide upturned moustache and a thin vertical pointed beard.

Today, the Guy Fawkes mask is the widely recognized symbol of the hacktivist group *Anonymous*. Mackintosh used the occasion of Guy Fawkes Night to light an enormous bonfire and recruit more members into his gang. He orchestrated most activities in the south part of the city. Inciting public disturbance was not foreign to them.

The Loyal Nine needed soldiers—insurgents. They convinced Mackintosh to put aside his local quarrels with Henry Swift and the North Enders gang to direct their hostilities towards opposing the British and the Stamp Act. *The enemy of my enemy is my friend*. Mackintosh, Swift and the hundreds of their gang members agreed to work together.

Per a letter on display at the Massachusetts Historical Society, Cyrus Baldwin, a local civil engineer, recounted the events of the morning of August 14. Bostonians were greeted by:

something so Rair as to draw the attention of almost the whole Town – it was no less than the Effigie of the Honourable Stamp Master of [the] Province hanging on one of the great Trees at the south end directly over the main street – behind him was a Boot hung up with the Devil Crawling out, with the Pitchfork in his hand, on the Effigie's Right arm was writ and sew'd on the letters AO [Andrew Oliver] – On his left arm was wrote these words 'It's a glorious to See a stamp-man hanging on a Tree' ... This Effigie hung in this manner alday ... the mob ... took the Image down, after the performance of some Cerimonies. It was brought through the main street to near Olivers Dock, and in less than half an hour laid it even with the ground then took timbers of the house and caryd 'em up on Fort Hill where they stamped the Image & timber & made a bonfire – the fuel faild. – they Immediately fell upon the stamp Masters Garden fence, took it up, stampd it and burnt it ... Not contented with this they proceeded to his Coach house took off the doars, stampd 'em & burnt 'em. – While they was doing this, the Sheriff began to read the proclamation for the mob to withdraw.

The Loyal Nine, with the assistance of their new alliance, conducted the first, large-scale opposition against the Stamp Act and, specifically, a Stamp

Master. It was well planned, directed at a specific target and perfectly executed. The Loyal Nine's rationale was simple: without Stamp Masters, the Act could not go into effect. John Dickinson, former president of the Delaware colony and known as the *Penman of the Revolution*, wrote the hanging of the effigy was "the most effectual and most decent Method of preventing the Execution of a Statute that strikes the Axe into the Root of the Tree."

Word of the defiance spread throughout the colonies. Incidents of protest had been occurring in other cities and towns from Fort Halifax in Maine to Charleston, but now force had been introduced as a tool of the masses.

On August 26, Andrew Oliver informed his fellow Stamp Master, Jared Ingersoll of Connecticut, of his intention to resign from his office:

Sir: The News Papers will sufficiently inform you of the Abuse I have met with. I am therefore only to acquaint you in short, that after having stood the attack for 36 hours – a single man against a whole People, the Government not being able to afford me any help during that whole time, I was persuaded to yield, in order to prevent what was coming in the night; and as I happened to give out in writing the terms of Capitulation, I send you a copy of them.

The activities of the Loyal Nine and their alliance were having the desired effect—the tax collectors were resigning out of fear. These Patriot mobs used tactics of fear, force, intimidation and violence to demonstrate against the Stamp Act, and they targeted pro-Stamp Act supporters and officials. The Loyal Nine organized these mobs by putting anti-Stamp Act pamphlets and signage all over the streets of Boston, and hanging effigies of public officials and others who supported the Stamp Act.

On November 1, the day enforcement of the Stamp Act was to begin; there appeared in a Boston newspaper a caricature by John Singleton Copley, entitled "The Deplorable State of America." The cartoon expressed the emotions of the citizens of Boston who felt intimidated by the revenue measure. The power of the press was behind the Loyal Nine.

Four days later, the citizens of Boston were greeted by an unusual scene—Ebenezer Mackintosh, leader of the South Enders, and Henry Swift, leader of the North Enders, two bitter rivals, were leading their men side-by-side down the streets of Boston. These were two opposing gangs that had gone at each other with clubs and knives on Guy Fawkes Day for as long as anyone could remember. The citizens were amazed and confused—what had happened? The answer became known as the *Union Feast*. Samuel Adams, with the assistance of John Hancock, organized a series of dinners and invited all *classes of men*, meaning the two mobs, to share a meal together.

Sir Francis Bernard, former governor of the Province of New Jersey, recalled in his writings that some of the Loyal Nine were present and *with Heart and Hands in flowing Bowls and bumping Glasses*, the Sons of Liberty were born!

The Loyal Nine kept up the pressure on the tax collectors. On the evening of December 16, Andrew Oliver received a notice from the Loyal Nine that his presence was requested at the Liberty Tree the next day to publicly resign his office of Stamp Master. The letter ended with the following caveat: "Provided you comply with the above, you shall be treated with the greatest Politeness and Humanity. If not..." The next morning, he sent for his friend John Avery, whom he hoped would act as an intermediary between himself and the Loyal Nine. Avery told him that it was too late—that the effigies were already prepared. Oliver then offered to resign at the courthouse but was told that would not be acceptable. Shortly before noon, Mackintosh appeared at his door for the purpose of escorting Oliver through the streets of Boston to the Liberty Tree. Because there was a heavy rain, Oliver was permitted to read his resignation from an upper window of a house next to the Liberty Tree.

Henry Bass described the Loyal Nine's involvement in his diary:

On seeing Messrs. Edes & Gill last mondays Paper, the Loyall Nine repair'd the same Evg. [December 16] to Liberty Hall, in order to Consult what further should be done respecting Mr. Oliver's Resignation, as what had been done heretofore, we tho't not Conclusive & upon some little time debating we apprehended it would be most Satisfactory to the Publick to send a Letter to desire him to appear under Liberty Tree at 12 oClock on Tuesday, to make a publick Resignation under Oath: the Copy of which the advertisement, his Message, Resignation & Oath you have Inclos'd. The whole affair transacted by the Loyall Nine in writing the Letter, getting the Advertisements Printed, which were all done after 12 oClock Monday night, the advertisements Pasted up to the amount of a hundred was all done from 9 to 3 oClock.

John Adams similarly recalled the events in his writings:

[They] gave me a particular Account of the

Proceedings of the Sons of Liberty on Tuesday last in prevailing on Mr. Oliver to renounce his office of Distributor of Stamps, by a Declaration under his Hand, and under the very Tree of Liberty, nay under the very Limb where he had been hanged in Effigy, Aug. 14, 1765. Their absolute Requisition of an Oath, and under that Tree, were Circumstances, extremely humiliating and mortifying, as Punishment for his receiving a Deputation to be a Distributor after his pretended Resignation, and for his faint and indirect Declaration in the News Papers last Monday.

One Monday evening in January of 1766, John Adams was invited by two members of the Loyal Nine—Thomas Crafts, the painter, and George Trott, the jeweler—to spend an evening with them and the rest of the Loyal Nine at a local distillery. Adams wrote:

I went, and was civilly and respectfully treated, by all Present. We had Punch, Wine, Pipes and Tobacco, Bisquit and Cheese etc... I heard nothing but such Conversation as passes at all Clubs among Gentlemen about the Times. No Plots, no Machinations. They chose a Committee to make Preparations for grand Rejoicings upon the Arrival of the News of a Repeal of the Stamp Act, and I heard afterwards they are to have such Illuminations, Bonfires,

Piramids, Obelisks, such grand Exhibitions, and such Fireworks, as were never before seen in America.

The following February, Adams was again invited by Thomas Crafts to attend the Monday gathering of the Loyal Nine, but this time in his writings he referred to the group as the *Sons of Liberty*:

Yesterday I wrote you a few lines, by Dr Tufts, informing you the Sons of Liberty desired your company at Boston ... on Monday next, because they want you to write those inscriptions that I mentioned to you when last at Boston; one in favor of Liberty, not forgetting the true-born sons, and another with encomiums on King George, expressive of our loyalty ...P.S. Destroy this after reading it.

On March 18, 1766, the British Parliament repealed the Stamp Act. The Loyal Nine had fulfilled their purpose. The proclamation read:

In this present Parliament assembled, and by the authority of the same, that from and after the first day of May, one thousand seven hundred and sixty-six, the above-mentioned Act, and the several matters and things therein contained, shall be, and is and are hereby repealed and made void to all intents and purposes whatsoever.

Over the next three years, the Loyal Nine became more commonly known by the moniker the

Sons of Liberty. In August 1769, seven of the original nine members attended the largest gathering held by the Sons of Liberty to date. They met at the Liberty Tree and offered several toasts, then they:

dined with 350 Sons of Liberty at [Lemuel] Robinsons, the Sign of Liberty Tree ... We had two Tables laid in the open Field by the Barn, with between 300 and 400 Plates, and an Awing of Sail Cloth overhead, and should have spent a most agreeable Day had not the Rain made some Abatement in our Pleasures. ... After Dinner was over and the Toasts drunk... we [sang] the Liberty Song. ... This is cultivating the Sensations of Freedom. There was a large Collection of good Company. Otis and Adams are politick, in promoting these Festivals, for they tinge the Minds of the People, they impregnate them with the sentiments of Liberty. They render the People fond of their Leaders in the Cause, and averse and bitter against all opposers.

According to the *Boston Gazette*, the forty-fifth and final toast made was *Strong Halters, Firm Blocks, and Sharp Axes to all such as deserve either*, followed by the discharge of a cannon and three cheers.

The insurgent activity of the Sons of Liberty continued over the years—some more famous than others, but all leading to a seminal moment. On

November 27, 1773, the first of three ships carrying chests of tea arrived in Boston Harbor. Members of the Sons of Liberty met at the Green Dragon Tavern and organized night patrols along the wharf to keep watch of the ships; others organized a series of meetings in the Old South Meetinghouse to discuss whether to confiscate the tea or destroy it. The patrols were in existence for nearly three weeks. Among those on duty one of those nights were three original members of the Loyal Nine—Henry Bass, Thomas Chase, and Benjamin Edes.

Peter Edes, the son of Benjamin Edes, wrote the following in a letter to his grandson:

I recollect perfectly well that, in the afternoon preceding ... the destruction of the tea, a number of gentlemen met in the parlor of my father's house, how many I cannot say ... I was not admitted into their presence ... They remained in the house till dark, I suppose to disguise themselves like Indians, when they left the house and proceeded to the wharves where the vessels lay. After they left the room I went into it, but my father was not there.

Benjamin Edes and Thomas Chase were two of the faux Indians who left to participate in the Boston Tea Party on the evening of December 16, 1773.

For a period of ten years following the formation

of the Loyal Nine, tensions between the British government and the colonists grew. As pressures built in America, chapters of the Sons of Liberty were formed all over the Thirteen Colonies, especially throughout New England, Virginia, and the Carolinas.

As the Sons of Liberty grew, so did their desire to adopt their own heraldry. Heraldry was used throughout history as a means to express a group's pride and loyalty. In 1767, the Sons of Liberty adopted a five red and four white vertical-striped flag as the group's formal standard. It became known as the Rebellious Flag and the nine stripes paid tribute to the Loyal Nine.

The leaders of the revolt, the Sons of Liberty, were faced with a chance to fundamentally change the course of America. They faced a choice—continue to live under tyranny or choose freedom. They chose freedom. By 1775, their opportunity became reality and the war for independence began. But the seeds of freedom were planted by nine brave Bostonians who had a vision and the courage to stand by their convictions—**The Loyal Nine.**

THANK YOU FOR READING SEEDS OF LIBERTY!

If you enjoyed it, I'd be grateful if you'd take a moment to write a short review (just a few words are needed) and post it on Amazon. Amazon uses complicated algorithms to determine what books are recommended to readers. Sales are, of course, a factor, but so are the quantities of reviews my books get. By taking a few seconds to leave a review, you help me out and also help new readers learn about my work.

Sign up to my email list to learn about upcoming titles, deals, contests, appearances, and more!

Sign up at BobbyAkart.com

VISIT my feature page at Amazon.com/Bobby-

Akart for more information on my other action-packed thrillers, which includes over forty Amazon #1 bestsellers in forty-plus fiction and nonfiction genres.

I'D BE HONORED if you'd read the BOSTON BRAHMIN SERIES available on Amazon in print, audio, and eBook formats. For an excerpt of THE LOYAL NINE, read on. Also, a critically important Appendix is available for you to read—the DECLARATION OF INDEPENDENCE and the CONSTITUTION.

Choose Freedom!

EXCERPT FROM THE LOYAL NINE
BOOK ONE IN THE BOSTON BRAHMIN SERIES

PROLOGUE

**Thanksgiving
Hanover Square
Boston, Massachusetts**

One by one, nine men entered through the front door of one of Boston's many taverns. The blowing snow on this early winter blast followed behind them but quickly melted under the heat of the large fire warming the patrons.

Benjamin Edes, the first to arrive, sat quietly in the corner, nursed his drink, and imperceptibly nodded to them as they entered. Each man was powerful in his own way. He had his own invaluable contribution to the cause they passionately shared.

For Edes, his role was that he wielded the power of the press and with it, the ability to shape public opinion. With his words, he was able to whip the people into a frenzy and draw the ire of the government he so vehemently opposed.

After the last of them entered, crossing quietly through the tavern, and disappearing through a nondescript wooden door toward the rear of the building, Edes finished his libation and lifted his hefty frame off the oak chair to join them. He caught the attention of the barkeep who knew his role —*warn them if their meeting was discovered.*

Then, he motioned to the evening's special guest who sat quietly on the other end of the tavern. The man joined Edes and followed him into a room filled with tobacco smoke, muffled voices, and the occasional sound of laughter—although this was far from a social occasion.

The group's meetings had been shrouded in secrecy for if their location was known, they would be arrested, or killed. Their professions were diverse. Two were in the liquor business while two more were in manufacturing. One was a ship's captain, and another was a jeweler. They were ordinary men pursuing an extraordinary cause.

Edes and Henry Bass, a cousin of a future President, had collaborated on various insurgent activities in protest of the government's overbearing tariffs and laws. Over time, they'd grown to respect one another even though they had political differences of their own.

During the prior six months, they'd conferred with likeminded neighbors and business associates. The group became close knit and found they shared a common love of country and freedom. At this meeting, agreements impacting the future of a nation would be reached and a revolution would be born.

"Welcome my friends," announced Edes as he entered the candlelit room. "Thank you for braving this early taste of winter."

Edes was greeted heartily and offered a pouch of tobacco for his pipe. He politely declined and took his seat at the head of the long, carved wood table. His guest, a young attorney of thirty years old, sat to his right. The man was Harvard educated and known for his taking up legal cases against the government. He had written several opinion pieces for Edes' newspaper and was considered an *up-and-comer* within the group's movement.

"Of course, Ben," said John Avery, the group's secretary. He kept notes of their meetings and established the agenda for future activities of the group.

"My wife was not particularly fond of a Thanksgiving meeting, but she understood the need."

Several members of the group nodded their agreement and toasted their mugs of ale. The goals of the nine men were lofty and could not be achieved without the support, as well as discretion, of their families.

"Good," started Edes. "Until now, we've operated as a group of nine. Tonight, that is about to change. I think all of you are acquainted with our guest this evening—John Adams."

"Welcome, John!"

"Cheers, my friend."

"Thank you for coming, Humphrey Ploughjogger!"

John Adams led the chorus of laughter as the men raised their mugs and toasted their guest. As Adams had become more notorious in his opposition to the tyrannical government's activity, he was increasingly harassed by those in power. He reprised his pen name, Humphrey Ploughjogger, to write four scathing articles about the government's heavy-handed approach in dealing with taxation and control of its citizens.

"Well, thank you for the hearty welcome and it's my honor to join the nine of you this evening," said

Adams. "I applaud all of you for your efforts in leading the opposition to tyranny. Like Ben Edes, I am a man of words—both written and spoken. Until now, they have served me well. But times have changed."

"How so, John?" asked George Trott, a jeweler.

Adams took a deep breath and responded. "George, there comes a time in history when words aren't enough. In order to effectuate change, our numbers must grow. Real change, whether in the form of a revolution or a declaration of independence, must necessarily require more active participants than the loyal nine men in this room. It requires groups like this one, but one-hundred-fold, from the Province of New Hampshire to Savannah in the south."

"What do you propose, John?"

"We must take our cause to the people and recruit likeminded individuals to assist us. Sacrifices must be made, and risks will be taken, but they are necessary to make us truly free, independent men."

Edes stood and walked to a table which held a plate of cigars. He chewed off the end and spit it on the floor. With the rolled tobacco extending out of his mouth, he leaned into a candle and lit it, allowing the smoke to billow to the ceiling before he rejoined his brethren.

"John, I sense you have more on your mind than recruiting men to start a revolution, am I right?"

"Yes, Ben. As freedom-loving patriots, we have big dreams of a country free of tyranny. I look at your faces and I know what's in your hearts. It's the same as the people who live throughout Boston and across this great land. But fighting for freedom is only the first part of the battle."

"What are you saying, John?"

"Liberty once lost, is lost forever. It is incumbent upon us, and our ancestors, to maintain the freedoms we earn out of our actions, which will necessarily require losses of life and property to obtain."

"We are all committed servants," said Edes. Several of the attendees toasted mugs and said *hear, hear*.

"Then, you must commit to an eternity of service, binding your families now, and your ancestors forever to the cause of opposing tyranny and maintaining the freedoms we desire. And gentlemen, you must pledge to take whatever actions necessary to live up to this commitment."

The group began to speak amongst themselves,

and their words grew louder within the room to the point where Edes had to bring them to order.

"Gentlemen, please," he said as they began to quieten down. Edes turned his attention back to Adams, the future second President of the United States. "John, please continue."

"Ben, tonight, we must submit our lives to politics and war, so that our families and all Americans will have the liberty to teach their children mathematics, philosophy, the arts, and the religion of their choosing. They should be able to speak their mind without fear of retribution. They should be able to read the opinions of others in the press without a tyrannical government stopping them.

"More importantly, we must maintain the virtue and spirit of us soon to be fledgling nation. Without the American spirit, the republic will be lost although it may still exist in its form."

Again, the nine men began to voice their opinions to one another. Avery, always intent on keeping notes for the group's meetings, tapped his mug on the table to bring the group to order. He turned his attention to Adams.

"John, you have stated that we should form a government of laws, and not of men. We all agree with you. What is the guiding principle that you are asking us to follow, so that we may impart the same upon our ancestors for generations?"

John Adams rose from his seat, tugged on the lapels of his coat, and looked at each of the nine men, one at a time. "It is quite simple. When faced with the choice between compromising our principles or choosing freedom—we should always choose freedom."

The year was 1765. The seeds of liberty were sown by The Loyal Nine, and a man who'd become known as one of the greatest orators for the cause of freedom the world had ever known.

PART 1

Over two hundred and fifty years later...

ONE

**December 15
Shirokino, Ukraine**

No warning preceded the artillery barrage. A sharp detonation shook the BTR-7 Defender, knocking the American halfway off the troop compartment bench, as fragments thunked against the armored personnel carrier's thin protective plate. Personal equipment and gear attached to the inside of the starboard-side hull popped loose, tumbling into the tight aisle.

He traded knowing looks with the Ukrainian Special Operations team assigned to escort him. There was nothing they could do to improve the situation. Combat was defined by probability and statistics, and they all knew what to expect next. The second round in the barrage would either land closer or farther from the vehicle, deciding their fate—and there was no way to hide from it.

The next explosion straddled the road, violently rocking the vehicle on its eight-wheel chassis. Fragments punctured the port-side hull, hissing and ricocheting through the armored coffin. The soldier seated to his right snapped backward against the vehicle's hard interior and slid motionlessly off the bench. Screams of pain pierced the compartment, quickly muted by successive high-explosive blasts. He tucked his knees into the metal bench, making room for the team's medic, who sprang into action from the back of the vehicle.

"This one is gone," the American said in broken Russian, lifting the dead soldier's black watch cap.

A jagged, charred hole appeared above his left eyebrow, evidence that a small red-hot fragment had passed through the wool hat and penetrated his skull. The Special Operations medic directed a flashlight beam at the grisly sight and nodded, pushing through the cramped compartment to reach the source of the screaming near the vehicle's turret. By the sound of the soldier's cries, the wound had to be severe. Special Operations soldiers had a predilection for suffering in silence, and this one was kicking and screaming.

The barrage lifted as quickly as it arrived, leaving them alone for the rest of the short ride to the Shirokino front. A few minutes later, after they had calmed the wounded soldier, the vehicle commander's voice echoed through the vehicle, spurring the soldiers into action. A pair of soldiers lifted the hatches above the troop compartment, squeezing their equipment-laden torsos through the openings. Shirokino was a fluid battlefront against pro-Russian separatist forces, and the vehicle commander wanted three-hundred-and-sixty-degree situational awareness as they approached their destination. Freezing rain sprayed through the hatches, driven by a brutal wind that had accompanied a rare Crimean weather front.

The vehicle slowed, and his escort team slid toward the starboard-side exit hatch. When the vehicle stopped, the soldiers opened the two-piece door, disappearing through the hull. The mercenary followed them into the driving rain, sprinting toward a series of drab, pockmarked Soviet-era buildings surrounded by barren trees. He stole a glance at the BTR-7 behind them, seeing two shredded tires. He'd always thought four tires on each side was overkill, but maybe the Soviets had been onto something with their original BTR design.

He kept pace with the commandos, stopping at a low-profile, earthen bunker just inside the tree line. Two serious-looking, heavily armed men wearing dark green camouflage uniforms and ballistic helmets greeted them at the sunken, heavy-wooden-beam-framed entrance to a reinforced defensive checkpoint. Splintered tree trunks and mangled branches gave him reason to believe the area was frequently targeted by separatist artillery. The cold rain was bad enough.

The gruff-looking soldiers fired a string of questions at the Ukrainian commandos, who rapidly answered and stepped aside. All he understood from the exchange was the word *Amerykans'kyy*. The Ukrainian and Russian languages didn't share enough in common to assure mutual intelligibility.

One of the soldiers asked another round of questions, clearly frustrating the Ukrainian commandos. The second soldier stared at him intensely, almost pathologically, as the rain streamed down his helmet.

"Is there a problem?" he said in Russian, hoping to break this little stalemate.

"Big problem. Our commander doesn't want to

meet with you today," said the psychotic-looking soldier.

"That's not what I was told an hour ago," he replied. "Good men have died bringing me here."

The man scoffed at the statement, causing a visible scowl from one of the Ukrainian commandos.

"You got a problem?" asked the soldier, nodding at the commando.

The Ukrainian Special Operations officer shook his head and muttered in Russian, loud enough for them to hear, "Militia scum." Instead of the lethal knife fight or point-blank gun battle he expected, the unstable-looking soldier took a step back and laughed.

"Well, this militia scum has liberated more territory in a month than the Ukrainian military has recaptured in a year," he said, motioning for him to step forward. "We'll return this guy after the meeting. Go on—before the separatists drop more shells on your head."

He nodded at the commando leader, who had been assigned to deliver him, unarmed and unharmed, to the Azov Battalion's forward headquarters in Shirokino. Andriy Biletsky, the ultranationalist founder and leader of the Azov Battalion, promised to meet with him during an inspection of the battalion's front-line positions. He would have much preferred to catch up with Biletsky in a quiet bar or swank restaurant in Kyiv, but the enigmatic leader had proven elusive and especially distrustful of foreign interests. His benefactors' research indicated that Biletsky's battalion was bankrolled exclusively by Ukrainian oligarchs, a sign of his ultranationalist loyalty.

His mission was to change that. The former Navy SEAL officer turned mercenary had been sent to make an offer his benefactors hoped Biletsky wouldn't refuse. It wouldn't be an easy sell. Azov Battalion had fought hard to recapture Mariupol from the pro-Russian rebels, pushing the separatists to the outskirts of Shirokino, where the battle had stalemated for months. His benefactors' offer of guaranteed, continued arms shipments and financial support came with a high price tag. A price tag he was afraid to mention.

"Follow me," said the soldier, motioning toward the building directly ahead of them. "He has a bunker beneath the building. You speak Russian, huh? *Amerykans'kyy* still study Russian?"

"Some enemies never change," said Nomad.

The man laughed, slapping him on the shoulder before heading toward the abandoned apartment block. As the two men drew closer to the structure, he could tell that the buildings had been subjected to sustained bombardment. The sturdy, four-story concrete testaments to Soviet construction stood unfazed despite extensive superficial damage to an otherwise featureless façade. Sturdy construction was about all these buildings had going for them, and in the end, it was all they needed. He seriously doubted any similarly sized building designed in the United States could have withstood this kind of high-explosive facelift.

He detected a sniper on the third floor, four windows from the corner; the faintest glare from the shooter's scope contrasted with the darkness of the room beyond the missing windowpane. He guessed the sniper was relatively inexperienced, possibly assuming that the rain and overcast skies would be enough to conceal him. Maybe to the untrained eye, but certainly not his. He'd started scanning for possible sniper hides as soon as his feet hit the frozen mud next to the armored vehicle.

"Inside that door," said the soldier, pointing to the blasted frame of a double-sized doorway in the middle of the ground floor. "Another group will escort you to the colonel. They're watching us."

He nodded and jogged toward the opening,

detecting movement inside the darkened entryway. He hated gigs like this. Multiple handoffs, different personalities—the perpetual feeling that you're one twitchy finger away from being shot in the face. Staring into the shadowy entrance, he had no doubt that more than one set of stone-cold killer eyes had already lined him up through the iron sights of an AK-74.

"Hello?" he yelled, cautiously approaching the abyss.

The distinctive whistle of a passing artillery shell replaced the silence, spurring one of the hidden militiamen to lurch out of the darkness and grab him by the jacket.

"Get inside, you idiot," the man grumbled, tossing him through the opening as he yelled, "Incoming!"

He stumbled over broken glass, striking a cinderblock wall several feet into the building. A pair of hands seized his shoulders from behind, steering him through a maze of dark hallways to a set of stairs lit by a hanging kerosene lantern. A soldier appeared inside the door leading into the hidden bunker, partially illuminated by the soft glow of the lantern.

"*Amerykans'kyy*," said his unseen escort.

"*Spasybi*, Vika, I'll take him from here," said the

soldier, instantly switching to classroom-taught English. "You're late. He's been waiting."

"We had to take a detour outside of Mariupol. The roads don't appear to be secure in this sector," said Nomad, sensing that he was finally talking to someone in charge.

"No kidding. We're anticipating a Russian-backed assault on Mariupol any day now. Russian Spetsnaz are roaming the countryside, creating havoc. The front line here is more or less a sham at this point. Whatever you have to say to the colonel better be quick. We're pulling the battalion back within the hour. Anton Teresenko, Colonel Biletsky's deputy subcommander," said the soldier, extending a hand.

"Nomad. I'll keep my proposal short and to the point," he said, accepting the man's solid grip.

"Good. He doesn't like foreigners, just in case you hadn't heard," said Teresenko.

"I don't blame him. They tend to get in the way of a nation's affairs," said Nomad.

"Follow me, and don't speak unless spoken to. The colonel's not in a good mood," he said, rapidly descending the stairs.

The corridor extending beyond the bottom of the stairwell was lit by randomly hung kerosene lamps, leaving shadowy gaps in the long, sterile hallway.

"Fallout shelter?" asked Nomad.

Teresenko chuckled as he responded. "Actually, it's a relic from the Cold War. The central building in every housing block was equipped with one of these. Local Communist Party officials received preferential placement in these coveted buildings. Even the adjacent buildings were considered upgrades. Can you imagine? The Soviets were geniuses in that respect."

A soldier in full-body-armor kit stepped out of a doorway several feet away, his rifle held in the low-ready position. He snapped to attention at the sight of Teresenko.

"At ease," said the deputy commander, releasing the soldier to his hiding spot.

"The colonel is fanatical about security. He's been attacked more times than any of us care to count," said Teresenko.

"I was a bit surprised to be X-rayed in Mariupol. Seemed a bit excessive," said Nomad.

"I would have thought the same thing four weeks ago, but Russian SVR agents in Donetsk forced a plastic surgeon to swap Semtex for silicon in an unsuspecting stripper's breast implants. The surgeon tipped off local authorities after somehow ducking SVR surveillance. The scumbags blew her up in her apartment, with the police right outside the door. We're not taking any chances," he said, pointing to the next doorway on the left. "That's our door."

He led Nomad inside a well-lit room occupied by several men in camouflage uniforms. He immediately recognized Biletsky standing in front of a large, wall-mounted map. Standing average height, he wore a black ball cap pulled tightly over his head. A scruffy, half-grown beard extended from the sides of his cap, ending in a goatee. He looked more like a millennial in a camouflage jacket than the leader of the Ukraine's fiercest, pro-nationalist militia group. The man's icy blue eyes portrayed a different story. As Teresenko suggested, he waited to be addressed.

"This better be good. I have more important things to do than play CIA games," said Biletsky, turning his attention back to the map.

"I'm not with the CIA," said Nomad.

"Everyone is working for the CIA, or the SVR, in one capacity or another," said Biletsky.

"I assume you received the money?" asked Nomad.

"You wouldn't be standing here if I hadn't. You

can thank the CIA for their kind donation to our cause," said Biletsky.

Kind donation? Two million dollars in an untraceable account was considered "kind" by Biletsky. This might be harder than he originally thought. What if his benefactors had been wrong in their assessment? The oligarchs had made generous donations to the Azov Battalion, but two million was supposed to be in line with current levels of private-sector support. If money didn't get Biletsky's attention, he'd have to change tactics.

"Can you hold Mariupol?" Nomad asked, deciding to take a more direct approach.

"Excuse me?" asked Biletsky, turning to face him.

"It's no secret that the Russians have stepped up activity around Mariupol. Can you hold the city?" he asked.

"I liberated that city from the separatists. I have no intention of losing it again," said Biletsky. "Is that all you have?"

"No. I have a dozen T-80 main battle tanks to donate to the Azov Battalion," said Nomad.

Biletsky cocked his head and walked around the map-strewn table, approaching him with a cold stare.

"Tanks?" he said.

"And a comprehensive training package, along with the necessary support vehicles to keep them running," said Nomad.

"I'm listening," said Biletsky, stopping a few feet in front of him.

"You're not going to like what I say next," said Nomad.

"No?"

"No. In order to get the tanks, you have to abandon Mariupol—"

Biletsky's eyes bored through him; the man's previously uncommitted gaze suddenly turned murderous.

"Temporarily," added Nomad. "And there's far more to this deal than tanks."

"Like what?" asked Azov Battalion's commander.

"The opportunity to destroy a Russian motorized infantry battalion, en masse, on Ukrainian soil, in front of the world," said Nomad.

"Now I'm really listening," said Biletsky.

TWO

December 15
Harvard Kennedy School of Government
Cambridge, Massachusetts

His students shuffled into their seats and unpacked the tools of their trade—computer tablets, voice recorders, various and sundry electronic gadgets—all designed to let them pay attention to their professor without fear of distraction or falling behind on the lecture.

"So, we find ourselves at the end. Last class of the semester," said the professor to a chorus of uplifting murmurs. "And finals will be on Tuesday." His patented kill shot transformed the positive mood as students throated their distaste for the reminder.

"Oh, I see how it is. Happy to see the last of me, but the thought of finals is the end of the world as we know it."

Laughter filled the classroom as the moods lifted. Professor Henry Winthrop Sargent IV, affectionately known as Sarge, once again wondered if the students' collective response meant they truly enjoyed his lectures—or the pleasure of his academic company paled in comparison to the terror of his final exam. He'd probably never know for sure, he thought, as the title of his final lecture appeared on the screen.

CYBER WARFARE
IS IT AN ACT OF WAR?

The words had a sobering effect on the muffled conversations in the room. While they absorbed the question of the day, Sarge looked at the faces and placards containing their names. Some of these people would be rich and powerful someday. The Harvard Kennedy School—John F. Kennedy School of Government—deserved the respect that its prestigious name implied. The school's history dated back to the late 1930s, but its rise to prominence came in 1966 when it was renamed for the late president John F. Kennedy.

The school's alumni list was a who's who collection of government leaders, journalism headliners and business aristocracy. Names like Ban Ki-moon, United Nations Secretary General; Paul Volcker, former chairman of the Federal Reserve; and outspoken talk show host Bill O'Reilly of Fox News fame. Even the president of Harvard, Lawrence Summers, a former professor at the Kennedy School, had been an economic advisor to the World Bank and United States presidents.

When Sarge was offered an academic position at the school, he had big shoes to fill—not exactly a problem for a direct descendant of Daniel Sargent, a wealthy merchant during the time of the Revolutionary War and a notable member of the memorable Sons of Liberty. This historical and financial lineage provided Sarge the necessary status to be considered for Harvard, where he received a Bachelor of Arts, combined with master's and doctorate degrees in public policy and government. It also didn't hurt that Sarge had important *friends*, most of whom he had never met. From an early age, Sarge understood that he had been groomed for his position as professor, on top of "other duties."

"The world has come a long way since the Minutemen fired the first shots at the Battles of Lexington and Concord in 1775. Today, cyber warfare is used by the military to attack less traditional battlefield prizes—command and control technology, critical national infrastructure systems and air defense networks, each of which require computer automation to operate."

"Prior to the Russian invasion of Ukraine," said Sarge with a facetious cough, eliciting some quiet laughter from the class. "I mean the separatist uprising. Russia followed a template that worked successfully during its invasion of Georgia in 2008. Ukraine experienced the same cyber chaos that wreaked havoc in Georgia before Russia rolled in with its tanks. The writing on the wall was literally written in the malicious computer code propagated throughout Ukraine.

"Before Crimea seceded to Russian control in early 2014, Kyiv was overwhelmed by a series of sophisticated and coordinated cyberattacks, crippling communications networks and shutting down government websites with denial-of-service attacks," Sarge continued, with the room's rapt attention.

"By the way, if you think that couldn't happen in the U.S., think again. Early this year in northern Arizona, *vandals* cut a critically sensitive fiber-optic cable, disrupting police and state government databases, banks, hospitals and businesses for several hours. No ATMs. No credit card transactions," he said, pausing. "And no Internet—heaven forbid."

The class laughed at this lighthearted jab at their generation.

"What I found interesting about all of these reports was that investigators used the terms *vandals or vandalism* repeatedly, implying a bunch of bored high school kids might be responsible; plausible? I don't think so. The fiber-optic cable was encased in a two-inch-thick steel pipe. Breaching this pipe would have required more than a simple hacksaw as reported. Even a battery-powered reciprocating saw might not do the trick. And yes, I did some research. These hands don't see the use of hacksaws very often," said Sarge, drawing more laughter.

"The question has to be asked: *Was the Arizona event a trial run for something bigger?* Is there a rogue nation or terrorist group contemplating an attack on the United States using the Russian template so successful in Georgia and Ukraine? Probably not, unless this starts happening more frequently. Time will tell. Fortunately for you, the new face of warfare might be a little clearer."

Sarge looked out into the classroom. When teaching, Sarge enjoyed having instructive dialogue with his students. He employed the Socratic Method, named for the Greek philosopher Socrates. Universally feared by law students, he employed a more productive version of Socrates' contribution to academia, asking question after question until the entire class came to a collective conclusion—no small feat when so many cultures and political points of view were represented in one room.

"Mr. Feltzer," said Sarge, bringing the young man to attention in his seat, "are you familiar with the cyberattack on Sony Pictures in 2014, which cost them nearly a billion dollars?"

"Yes, sir," replied Feltzer.

"Was this an act of war?" asked Sarge.

"No, sir," replied Feltzer.

"Well, I agree, although I believe if Sony Pictures had real cannons, they would have found somebody to shoot," said Sarge, to a room of laughter. "In fact, the President made a point in a CNN interview to call the attack *cyber-vandalism*."

He strolled along the front of the room, studying the young minds soaking in his words.

"Ahhh," continued Sarge, "there's that word again—vandalism. An attack upon the private sector that results in economic loss does not give rise to an act of war. Would everyone agree with that statement as our first premise?" Sarge observed heads nodding all around.

"Thank you, Mr. Feltzer. Miss Crepeau, you're up," said Sarge.

The young woman who sat in the front row was eager to jump into the discussion, as always, thought Sarge. Sarge recognized from day one he had to be careful with *that one*.

"Let's continue with the *Russian Template*, as we'll call it. I have a hypothetical for you, Miss Crepeau. We have already discussed the vandals who cut the fiber-optic cable in Arizona. What if these *vandals* simultaneously, via a cyber attack, took down Tucson Electric and the Salt River Project that services Phoenix? Now do we have an act of war?" asked Sarge.

"Not yet," she replied. "Although these acts are coordinated by these vandals, there has not been sufficient corresponding death and destruction to warrant military action."

"How many deaths?" asked Sarge.

"Excuse me?" she replied.

"For all of you," said Sarge, addressing the entire class, "how many deaths from this type of coordinated attack would warrant a military response?" As Sarge looked around the class, he heard responses of *hundreds, thousands* and *just one is enough.*

"Thank you, Miss Crepeau. Therein lies the rub," said Sarge, quoting *Hamlet.*

"I heard answers ranging from one to several thousand. The challenge for any government is to identify a standard—a breaking point—that requires a nation to go to war," said Sarge.

"For most governments, the standard is vague and leaves a lot of wiggle room. By the way, that is a global governance term of art—*wiggle room,*" said Sarge to a few stifled laughs.

"Officially, both the White House and the Pentagon consider a cyberattack emanating from a foreign country an act of war. But they do not spell out when a cyberattack is serious enough to constitute an act of war. As Miss Crepeau suggests, I suspect a cyberattack that produces death, damage and destruction similar to a traditional military attack might merit retaliation through the use of force," concluded Sarge.

Sarge had set them up, just as Socrates would have in the fifth century B.C. The class now seemed to agree death and destruction was a prerequisite to military retribution. *Let's twist them around a little, starting with the law student.*

"Mr. Robbins, let me begin with you," said Sarge. "Did you agree with the consensus of the class that the cyberattack on Sony Pictures was not an act of war?"

"Yes, sir, I did," responded Robbins authoritatively.

"Mr. Robbins, do you believe that a coordinated cyberattack could devastate the U.S. economy?" asked Sarge.

"It would depend on the severity and what systems were affected. Professor, would you consider it an act of war if the Sony Pictures attack was made in conjunction with a shutdown of the stock market?" asked Robbins, Socratically.

Well done, lawyer-to-be. You answered a question with *it depends* and threw it back at me with another question of clarification.

"Let's look at a real-world example, shall we?" asked Sarge.

"In 2007, once again, our friends the Russians," said Sarge with his voice trailing off. "After today, I'm sure to have my travel privileges to Russia suspended. He continued.

"In 2007, the tiny country of Estonia mistakenly poked the Russian bear by moving a controversial Soviet-era memorial from the town square in Tallin to a remote location. The large Russian minority in Estonia protested, as did the Russian government. For weeks thereafter, Estonia businesses and utilities suffered a barrage of cyber attacks that brought the private sector to a screeching halt.

"While the Estonia attacks were not the largest on record, they were sufficient to bring a country considered to be especially *wired* to its knees. The resulting recession was considered a direct result of the cyberattacks," said Sarge.

"The Gross Domestic Product of the United States economy is eighty percent services. In economic terms, a service is an intangible commodity. Any event that disrupts the ability of those services to be rendered will necessarily result in a downturn of the economy. For example, according to a Department of Commerce report, the economic losses caused by Superstorm Sandy, a storm event lasting twenty-four hours, totaled one hundred billion dollars."

"Mr. Robbins, if a rogue nation, via a cyberattack, caused economic losses in this country totaling one hundred billion dollars, would that be an act of war?" asked Sarge.

"No, sir. If I were president, and one day I will be, only significant loss of life warrants a war response," said Robbins.

"Mr. President-to-be, I will submit there have been many wars fought over a lesser economic impact than the hypothetical we have described, and I suspect we will see this scenario play out in our lifetimes," said Sarge.

"I'm going to conclude this semester with a teaser for the companion course that will start in January." Sarge changed the screen.

GLOBAL GOVERNANCE
+
ECONOMIC POLICY

"For years, U.S. officials have dismissed the need for international negotiations and cooperation on cyberspace, but now appears to be in the process of collaborating with our allies to develop rules for the virtual world. The trend appears to be headed toward the creation of cyber policy, including establishing a threshold where a cyber attack constitutes an act of war. This trend reflects the growing sentiment that our domestic efforts to secure cyberspace are inadequate. We will study whether the impact on the U.S. economy is driving this change in the government's approach," said Sarge, bringing up the final slide for the day.

FINAL TUESDAY
12/18/15

The collective grumbles in the background were lost on Sarge as he gathered his notes from the lectern. Sarge replaced the cap on his Mont Blanc pen and tucked it away in his shirt. An uneasy feeling of dread and foreboding hit him, casting his mind adrift.

THREE

December 15
73 Tremont Street

Donald Quinn waited patiently at the traffic light, preparing to turn left onto Tremont Street. Before him, he observed the northeast corner of Boston Common—all but deserted in the winter. Joggers, tourists and leaves had all gone into hibernation, taking the vitality of this historic city space with them. In the summer, the pedestrian circle was filled with passersby swarming the locally famous Donut Cart or Giuseppe's Italian Ice. There weren't many patrons for Italian Ice in mid-December. Despite his new training regimen, Donald might have splurged on a bag full of arepas, which was a corn pocket stuffed with a variety of savory fillings, a staple in South America. But, alas, even the warm offerings had flown south for the winter.

After parking the *jalopy*, as Mrs. Quinn teasingly called his 1972 Jeep CJ5 Renegade, Donald began his trek up the hill toward 73 Tremont. Now painted flat black, Donald chose this vehicle as his *company car*. Sure, he had his pick of the litter. As the *Director of Procurement*, any flashy vehicle was an option, but the only flash that concerned him was an electromagnetic pulse bomb detonated over the good ole U.S. of A.

When he showed Susan his choice, she understood the reasoning. However, *for appearances,* she said, her choice would be something more conventional—a Cadillac Escalade. Donald thought his choice was a wise one, despite her misgivings. The Renegade was obscure and undistinguished, blending into society unnoticed—as did Donald.

Donald was new to the preparedness lifestyle, having only embraced the concept in the last six or seven years. It started with an unsolicited novel by William Forstchen, followed by a series of books in the genre sent to him by Susan. The concepts in the books struck a chord, and he began to perceive world events differently. He became a student of prepping and devoured every book and preparedness guide available on the subject.

He and Susan married in 2005 with a well-attended wedding. Susan had just completed her military career in the Air Force, and Donald was firmly ensconced at the accounting firm of Vitale Caturano—VC. Although they were not Big Four, VC was one of the most prestigious firms in Boston, boasting an international clientele. Donald, the consummate accountant, was of average height, stocky and relatively nondescript. Susan, a devout Christian and the daughter of a wealthy Bostonian with roots dating back to the Lowells, loved him dearly. Soon after marriage, life took an interesting and unexpected turn.

Upon taking their wedding vows, Donald and Susan envisioned a simple life. Good jobs, a two-car garage, two kids and the requisite Labrador retriever. Instead, Donald *took one for the team*. In 2009, with a three-year-old wreaking havoc on the Quinn household and another child on the way, Donald plead guilty to seven counts of a federal indictment, to include charges of money laundering and conspiracy to commit income tax evasion.

VC's client list consisted of many wealthy, connected Bostonians, all requiring complex tax, estate and retirement planning. Donald was tasked with assisting a friend of his father-in-law with his estate plan, despite his relative inexperience with estate plans of this magnitude. His new client was adamantly opposed to the concept of federal estate taxes, particularly the newly proposed changes to the inheritance tax. Further, he was concerned with protecting his assets from an ex-wife, who had openly voiced that she was entitled to his estate—because she had "paid her dues."

Unknown to Donald, the client had already made several ill-advised attempts at financial planning, which included large transfers of money to exotic locales like the Turks and Caicos Islands, Tortola, and Nevis. How the client was able to transfer several million dollars to the banks in these countries was never fully disclosed to Donald.

One evening, Donald returned to their home in Waltham to a welcoming committee that would alter the course of his life. Present were his visibly shaken and very pregnant wife, his father-in-law Charles

Lowell, the client, and a mystery guest—an older gentleman who was never formally introduced and remained silent during the entire meeting.

Within an hour, Donald agreed to plead guilty to the federal charges, taking full responsibility for the client's ill-advised scheme. Despite the magnitude of the crime, Donald was assured that he would receive no more than a twenty-four-month sentence. The plea agreement had already been negotiated. With good time, he would return home within twenty-one months—to a new house in Brae Burn Country Club in West Newton, a guaranteed high six-figure income, and a position dealing in large part with the *Mystery Man*. Susan kept her composure throughout the meeting, smiling reassuringly with the occasional tear. She was a real soldier.

Donald reported directly to the Federal Medical Center on the grounds of Fort Devens, just forty-five minutes west of Boston, where he was immediately assigned a serious medical condition—despite being in perfect health. All part of the complex illusion of his incarceration, he would discover.

What immediately struck Donald was the fact there were no fences or guard towers surrounding FMC. It looked like any other group of buildings. Over time he realized why they called this type of facility a *country club*. It wasn't the Brae Burn lifestyle that awaited him, but it certainly beat a federal penitentiary. Mystery Man couldn't buy Donald's way out of prison, but he could apparently purchase a medical condition—the next best thing in the Federal Bureau of Prisons. His condition came with perks.

Ordinarily, any other inmate would miss many of the life-changing events on the outside like the birth of a child. Not Donald. He was whisked away on a "medical emergency," requiring outside medical treatment, for the birth of their second daughter, and was allowed to stay with Susan for a couple of nights.

Despite being away from Susan and the girls most of the time, Donald changed for the better during his stay at FMC Fort Devens. He started to exercise regularly, replacing thirty pounds of fat with lean muscle in the facility's weight room. Donald also became a prepper, reading every book sent to him and taking detailed notes.

Donald's final wake-up inside FMC was little more than a physical formality. His mind had already been awakened and conditioned with a different view of the world. The memories of his time away from Susan were a constant reminder of how his life had changed, and the opportunities which opened up as a result of the sacrifice he made. With a renewed sense of purpose, Donald confidently walked up Tremont Street for a meeting with his *benefacto*r, curious as to what the day might bring.

FOUR

December 15
Boston, Massachusetts

Sarge bounded down the front steps of the Belfer Center like a kid released for summer break—only to be greeted with a brisk winter breeze and an MBTA bus roaring down Eliot Street. The temperatures were already far milder than the previous year, spurring hope they might avoid a repeat of the one hundred plus inches of snowfall that wreaked havoc in the eastern United States. A cold breath of air, supplemented with the exhaust of the MBTA bus, was a welcome relief from hundred-car pileups on the highways and scenes of downed power grids in Tennessee.

He resisted the urge to run into Dunkin' Donuts, opting instead for a quick cash withdrawal at the Bank of America ATM. Long lines inside the branch caught his attention. *Odd for closing time on a Tuesday; maybe everybody is going Christmas shopping.*

Part of Sarge's *duties and responsibilities*, in addition to his profession, was to keep up with world events, especially related to global economics. As he shoved the twenties into his pocket, he thought about how worthless these paper notes might become someday. Today's modern banking system manufactured money out of thin air. Like a magician's sleight of hand, global bankers had the power to create money and control credit markets. With the stroke of a pen or the punch of a keyboard, they could deliver wealth to whomever they chose.

Ironic, Sarge thought to himself as he pressed the key fob on his new Mercedes-Benz G63 AMG. *Am I hypocritical to condemn the activities of the global elite, the same powerful people who provided this G-Wagen to me as a company car?* As he settled in, the earthy smell of the Nappa leather refocused him on the task at hand—Christmas shopping.

Sitting behind the heated steering wheel of the G63 was like entering the cockpit of an airplane. Having taken delivery just a few days ago, Sarge hadn't taken the proper time to familiarize himself with the interior. Starting the engine was the easy part. Then he adjusted all of the comfort features, which fortunately included lots of heating elements. Finally, of course, the ultimate in driver distraction was the G63's COMAND system with an 80 GB hard drive navigation system, Bluetooth, HDTV and Sirius radio. No wonder Apple and Google developed self-driving cars. Sarge would never use all of these gadgets. His rare 1968 Toyota OJ40, Bandeirante model, was more his speed. No frills, no thrills. The only thing these two vehicles had in common was a Mercedes-Benz engine. No fancy electronics in the Bandeirante, he thought. *That might be a good thing someday.*

Pulling out of the garage onto Eliot, he fumbled with the COMAND system and nearly struck the back tire of a bicycle—the backpack and winter coat laden student long gone by the time Sarge took a deep breath and exhaled. *See! This is what I'm talking about.* Finally getting his mind straight, Sarge managed to navigate south onto JFK without taking out any of the Kennedy School of Government's student body. An adjustment of the COMAND volume brought the voice of his friend Neil Cavuto to life.

"*Markets closed flat today amid continued uncertainty about whether Greece, Italy and Spain would reach bailout agreements with Eurozone officials. After the markets closed, a rumor swirled that a tentative agreement had been reached, which sent DOW futures higher. However, conflicting reports out of Frankfurt made by Deutsche Bank officials said otherwise, driving futures back to a negative position.*

"To discuss all of this, I have as my guest Jon Wellington with Barclays UK in London, how are you, sir?" asked Cavuto.

"*I am chipper as usual, Neil, and glad to be on with you this evening,*" said Wellington.

"*What do you make of this news, and how does it affect the markets?*" asked Cavuto.

"*All day long it was like watching a classic Wimbledon tennis match of troubles, with investors volleying between radio silence from a closed-door meeting amongst Eurozone leaders on the Mediterranean members and the brightening outlook of a cease-fire agreement in Ukraine. Markets would push higher on the positive reports out of Ukraine and then *fall lower on the uncertainty surrounding the Eurozone trio of trouble—Spain, Greece and Italy. Add to that a late-day press conference from the President regarding his use of executive powers and you had one bloody day of jittery stock trading,"* said Wellington.

"So what should investors consider as a plan of action?" asked Cavuto.

"Neil, markets like stability. As we have seen over the last five to six years, despite relatively sluggish growth worldwide, markets have risen to tremendous heights. Unfortunately, we are one bad news story away from deflating this incredible run for stocks," said Wellington.

"I'm a 'glass half full' kinda guy, Jon. What would you suggest for those of us who espouse to the 'glass half empty' outlook on investing?" asked Cavuto.

"In my experience, a 'glass half empty' investor is typically cautious and is likely to sell at the slightest hint of a market downturn. Then there are those few daredevil opportunists who fearlessly attack a potential downturn to turn a healthy profit. They short sell," said Wellington.

Sarge was travelling south on Soldiers Field Road along the River Charles, enthralled by this conversation. His job duties did not require managing investments. Those responsibilities fell on the shoulders of others. But it was important for him to understand the mechanisms of the markets and how it affected the geopolitical landscape. He passed Boston University, home of Rhett the Wet Noodle Terrier. *Lame-ass mascot.* He turned his attention back to the conversation.

"Short selling," continued Wellington, "*is the sale of a stock the seller does not own but has merely borrowed. It may sound like an odd practice, but it is actually done often by seasoned investors. Short selling is typically prompted by speculation or by a desire to hedge downside risk. It is a risky proposition for the average investor and is only recommended it be used by experienced traders who are familiar with the great financial risks.*"

"*Is now a good time to short sell?*" asked Cavuto.

"*Neil, no investor has a crystal ball. For the last several years, financial pundits have warned that the financial markets are overvalued and the central banks of the world, like the Federal Reserve, are out of bullets to deal with a financial crisis. Yet the markets keep rising. This meteoric rise is probably a function of all-time-low interest rates. Investors are willing to gamble their money in stocks rather than receive little or no interest in banking-related investments. But, to answer your question, in the absence of a 'bad news story' I referenced earlier, equities are still the way to go!"* said Wellington.

Sarge thought to himself—investing like a bunch of drunks. *They have no idea.*

FIVE

December 15
73 Tremont Street
Boston, Massachusetts

Donald crossed Tremont Street and walked purposefully up the sidewalk toward the Park Street intersection. Parking was available at 73 Tremont, but Donald made it a habit to park off-site on his rare visits to the *Penthouse*. Donald believed in maintaining some semblance of a gray-man strategy, especially when meeting with his benefactors. Better to blend in with other visitors to the building.

Waiting on the traffic to clear the crosswalk, he admired the historic Park Street Church across the boulevard. Despite his lack of historic bloodline, which flowed through the veins of his *benefactors*, Donald was an avid Revolutionary-era historian. He and Susan had long ago graduated from the touristy Freedom Trail, which included well-known attractions like the Old North Church, the USS *Constitution* and the site of the Boston Massacre. They now explored a lesser known, but equally important layer of history that blanketed Boston.

Crossing the street, Donald checked his watch, noting that he was early. *I insist on punctuality*—the words rang in Donald's head. He *insisted* on a lot of things. Beyond the curb, a tour guide dressed in the cold-weather version of traditional eighteenth-century garb began his presentation. Donald took a moment to listen. Despite its distinction as one of the Freedom Trail's most prominent features, the Park Street Church was a historic gem that never grew old.

"Welcome, everyone, and thank you for daring the brisk weather to continue on the Freedom Trail tour. I see most of you stretching to look skyward at the magnificent steeple, which sits atop the historic Park Street Church here on Tremont Street. By the way, did you know Tremont is always pronounced *trem-mont* in Boston, not *tree-mont*?" asked the guide.

Heads nodded affirmatively, although Donald suspected none of them knew this until now.

"Rising toward the heavens, the two-hundred-seventeen-foot steeple, designed by architect Peter Banner, was once the first landmark travelers saw when approaching Boston. Today, the first landmark a traveler sees is a series of illuminated road signs reading 'forty-five-minute delay on the Mass Turnpike.' Things have changed, have they not, my friends?" asked the guide, to hearty laughter.

"Built in 1809, the church took a prominent role in the abolishment of slavery. Speakers came from all over New England to advance their mission of human rights. On July 4th, 1831, the patriotic song 'My Country, 'Tis of Thee,' written by Samuel Francis Smith, was sung a capella during a children's Independence Day celebration," said the guide.

Passing the tourists' parked carriage—a red Hop-On, Hop-Off Trolley Bus—Donald continued up *trem-mont,* humming the words of the famous song.

"My country, 'tis of thee, Sweet land of liberty, Of thee I sing; Land where my fathers died, Land of the pilgrims' pride, From every mountainside, Let freedom ring."

If only that were still true. He somehow doubted the Founding Fathers would recognize the state of the republic they had left behind for the American people. Donald pushed his way through the impeccably polished, brass revolving door, pausing to wonder what would happen if he did a 360 and drove home. Nothing good.

Entering the lobby, Donald was struck by the magnificence of *la grande entrée* of 73 Tremont. After a major renovation in 1988 added several stories to the existing neoclassical granite structure, the building took on a character of its own. From the Carrara marble inlay floors to the forty-foot-tall, vaulted ceilings, the lobby was gracefully appointed with polished brass, mahogany wood and elegant soft lighting. Despite a level of grace and style that would rival the finest five-star hotel, the lobby was sparsely decorated to minimize the chance of an impromptu street gathering. Everything in 73 Tremont had been designed with a purpose.

Replacing the historical bellhops of the former Tremont House were subtle reminders of the buildings twenty-four-hour armed security team. A careful look revealed numerous security cameras shrewdly incorporated into the architectural finishes—an odd feature for a building owned by a trust set up to benefit Suffolk University. Of course, Donald knew all too well that the building had little to do with the university.

"Good morning, sir, how may we help you?" asked a well-dressed concierge behind the reception desk.

Donald could feel the eyes studying him from above. *I am not paranoid, just aware.*

"Yes, I have an appointment on the thirteenth floor," said Donald.

Two members of the building's security team emerged from a shallow alcove to Donald's right. *Men in Black* types. Definitely not your typical campus security arrangement.

"Your name, please?" asked the concierge, picking up a phone receiver.

Donald provided his name and waited several seconds. He wasn't sure why they put him through this drill. They'd probably identified him a block away. The concierge listened to the phone and nodded, replacing the receiver. Two more men emerged from the alcove, bringing the total to five.

"Before these gentlemen escort you upstairs, sir, we must ask if you are carrying any weapons—including sharp objects. If you have any weapons, please allow us to check them for you," said the concierge.

Donald had received his concealed-carry weapons permit shortly after his release from prison. He had never owned a gun prior to "going away," but it soon became clear his new job duties would require personal protection. Within weeks of returning, he received correspondence from the Office of the Pardon Attorney in Washington, D.C., granting him a full Article II pardon and restoration of his civil rights, permitting gun ownership. An application to the Massachusetts Parole Board, marked *APPROVED*, arrived a few weeks later, completing the process. Everything had been prearranged on his behalf. He'd never seen the applications.

"Yes, I do have a weapon to *check*," said Donald.

The concierge motioned for him to follow the men through a door, where he voluntarily surrendered his Springfield XD-S 9mm to the solemn gentlemen who hadn't smiled—much less spoken. One of the security team members released the magazine and cleared the chamber before locking it away in a wall safe. After a brief search of his Hartmann signature tweed briefcase, they motioned for him to follow. Although Donald had been through this procedure a few times before, it never failed to reinforce the importance of the man he had come to see.

Three members of the security crew entered the elevator. One of them inserting a key into an unnumbered slot on the brass elevator keypad. They rode to the thirteenth floor in awkward silence. When the elevator opened, Donald strode confidently to the reception desk, which was hosted by two attractive, professionally dressed women. On closer inspection, Donald could see how they trained their eyes on him—no doubt performing a threat assessment. He suspected their security training equaled, if not exceeded the men escorting him. Though it had been several months since Donald's last visit to the top floor of 73 Tremont, he felt an increased security presence. One of the women broke eye contact to glance at one of his escorts, who simply nodded. *Do they have mental telepathy too?*

"Just one moment, Mr. Quinn," she said, never taking her eyes off him again.

Pushing a button on her desk, she spoke softly into a wireless microphone attached to her jacket collar. "Mr. Quinn is here to see you, sir."

The male escorts stepped back to flank the elevator while one of the women circled the desk. She pointed to an intricately carved set of mahogany doors at the end of the reception hallway. *This is new.* He took in the details of the woodwork. Sheep and sheepdog on a hillside. Donald searched for the meaning, knowing these functional works of art had been purposely commissioned. The security guard opened the right door before he could form a theory.

"This way, please," she instructed, leading him past a wide bank of windows.

Of the many incredible views of Boston from the city's high-rise buildings, none matched the view west across Boston Common from the top floor of 73 Tremont. From the thirteenth floor's unique vantage point, one could also observe the Charles River, Commonwealth Avenue and the Massachusetts State House on Beacon Hill. The State House was particularly spectacular in the late afternoon, with the setting sun reflecting off the State House's twenty-three-karat gilded gold-leaf dome. The dull winter scene blazed to life, drawing the viewer's attention away from the bare trees and naked sidewalks directly below.

Opening another mahogany door, she motioned for him to enter his host's office—the inner sanctum. With slight trepidation, Donald stepped into a world out of reach for most. Measuring more than forty feet wide, the office was bigger than most Americans' homes. Gas fireplaces flanked both ends, rising through the two-story ceiling. The furnishings consisted of oriental carpets, dark chestnut furniture and overstuffed chairs, more resembling a gentlemen's lounge than an office. On the broad leather inlay desk centered in the middle of the room, two crystal glasses sat beside an opened bottle of Perrier.

Donald stood silently, waiting for the man standing in front of a set of velvet-clad French doors to acknowledge him. Appearing deep in thought, his benefactor finally spoke.

"Hello, Mr. Quinn, thank you for coming," he said, in the New England accent associated with people of aristocracy.

"Yes, sir, it is a pleasure to see you again," said Donald. *Not that I had a choice.*

He didn't expect the pleasantries to last for too long. The meeting had been hastily arranged. Something was brewing.

"I trust you have everything you need for your various projects," he said.

"Yes, sir, and I hope my reports are satisfactory," said Donald.

Donald always remembered to choose his words deliberately and concisely.

"Of course. Mr. Quinn, you will need to

take care of something for me—immediately following the close of the markets today," he said. "There are a number of transactions to be made, and you must use the highest levels of discretion."

I knew it; this couldn't be trusted to a phone call. Donald retrieved a small Louis Vuitton notebook from his suit jacket pocket.

"Immediately following this meeting, you are to execute the following transactions," said Donald's benefactor.

Listening intently, Donald took meticulous notes. The instructions represented the largest series of transactions he had executed to date. Donald had established a complex network of international brokerage accounts, which enabled him to effect secretive transactions—but never anything of this magnitude. *He knows something.* Donald jotted down country names in the left margin—Cook Islands, Dominica, St. Kitts, Turks and Caicos Islands.

The intricacy of the trades was significant, but not nearly as noteworthy as the sums of money involved over one billion dollars. *This would take days.*

"Mr. Quinn, this must be completed before the

opening of the Asian markets," he said, jarring Donald's attention from the notebook.

"Sir, I believe it is roughly five in the morning in Tokyo. Their markets open in about four hours. The New Zealand and Australian markets open an hour sooner, in roughly three hours," said Donald.

"Mr. Quinn," he said sternly, "you are prepared for this, are you not?"

Donald felt flush, taking a moment to respond carefully.

"Yes, sir, I have the systems and procedures in place. It's the scale of the transactions that concerns me," said Donald. "Currency trades of this magnitude will have repercussions throughout the global financial system. Although I have total confidence in the structure, I have established for you, there is also the possibility of enhanced scrutiny from the Commodity Futures Trading Commission. Taking a six-hundred-million-dollar short position in the euro, coupled with a six-hundred-million-dollar long position in the dollar, will wreak havoc in the equities markets as well." *And I'd rather not return to jail, regardless of how comfortable you can make my stay.*

His concerns rose above the scrutiny of the CFTC. The FOREX market was the largest foreign exchange market in the world, with currency changing hands continuously—but the size of these trades would rival the currency manipulations of George Soros. The potential upside was beyond contemplation—*more than a billion dollars.*

"Mr. Quinn, I have thought through this request thoroughly, and I am fully aware of the potential for international examination. Nevertheless, you will move forward. In addition, you are to short sell all of my positions in the following equities," he said, listing nearly a dozen U.S. and European companies. He said *all*. Donald quickly did the math—another four hundred million.

"Yes, sir," was all Donald could muster.

"I will have you escorted to an office, where you can execute my directives. A secure line is available, and you will have the complete assistance of a member of my staff if needed. Do you have any questions, Mr. Quinn?"

Yeah, what the hell do you know that nobody else does?

"No, sir," replied Donald.

Donald rose to leave. He took one more glance at his surroundings. *So, this is how you pay for this stuff?*

As if reading Donald's thoughts, his benefactor added, "I hope your wife and children are doing well."

Oh yes, very well, thanks to you, sir.

"They are sir. I thank you for the very generous gift on the birth of our daughter. She will benefit from a Harvard education," said Donald.

"You're welcome, Mr. Quinn. There is no substitute," he said, turning his attention to the view of Boston Common.

That was it. He was dismissed. Donald let himself out without another word and was escorted by a young man to a conference room on the other side of the thirteenth floor. The room was well appointed, featuring a full bar and six wall-mounted televisions.

"May I offer you anything to drink?" asked the young man.

Donald smiled and nodded. With the delivery of the Evian, the young man closed the door and left him alone. He took a quick inventory of the tools at his disposal. Telephones. Old school, but no doubt filtered by the securest encryption technology available. He pulled a chair in front of the phones and thought about Susan and the girls for a moment. They were extremely happy together as a family. Did their happiness come with a heavy price tag? Currency trading was practiced every day, right? *Not $1.2 billion at once, followed by another $400 million* *in stock manipulations. What did it matter? Forget the dollar amounts, make the trades and go home to your family.*

He pulled off his jacket and flung it into an empty chair. Unbuttoning and rolling up his sleeves, Donald executed the first in a series of steps that would make front-page news tomorrow morning.

THANK YOU for reading Seeds of Liberty. We invite you to purchase your copy of The Loyal Nine, Book One in The Boston Brahmin Series on Amazon, by clicking:

THE BOSTON BRAHMIN SERIES
Go back to Contents

DECLARATION OF INDEPENDENCE

IN CONGRESS, JULY 4, 1776

The unanimous Declaration of the thirteen United States of America

When in the Course of human events it becomes necessary for one people to dissolve the political bands which have connected them with another and to assume among the powers of the earth, the separate and equal station to which the Laws of Nature and of Nature's God entitle them, a decent respect to the opinions of mankind requires that they should declare the causes which impel them to the separation.

We hold these truths to be self-evident, that all men are created equal, that they are endowed by their Creator with certain unalienable Rights, that among these are Life, Liberty and the pursuit of

Happiness. — That to secure these rights, Governments are instituted among Men, deriving their just powers from the consent of the governed, — That whenever any Form of Government becomes destructive of these ends, it is the Right of the People to alter or to abolish it, and to institute new Government, laying its foundation on such principles and organizing its powers in such form, as to them shall seem most likely to affect their Safety and Happiness. Prudence, indeed, will dictate that Governments long established should not be changed for light and transient causes; and accordingly, all experience hath shewn that mankind are more disposed to suffer, while evils are sufferable than to right themselves by abolishing the forms to which they are accustomed. But when a long train of abuses and usurpations, pursuing invariably the same Object evinces a design to reduce them under absolute Despotism, it is their right, it is their duty, to throw off such Government, and to provide new Guards for their future security. — Such has been the patient sufferance of these Colonies; and such is now the necessity which constrains them to alter their former Systems of Government. The history of the present King of Great Britain is a history of repeated injuries and usurpations, all having in direct object the establishment of an absolute Tyranny over these States. To prove this, let Facts be submitted to a candid world.

He has refused his Assent to Laws, the most wholesome and necessary for the public good.

He has forbidden his Governors to pass Laws of immediate and pressing importance, unless suspended in their operation till his Assent should be obtained; and when so suspended, he has utterly neglected to attend to them.

He has refused to pass other Laws for the accommodation of large districts of people, unless those people would relinquish the right of Representation in the Legislature, a right inestimable to them and formidable to tyrants only.

He has called together legislative bodies at places unusual, uncomfortable, and distant from the depository of their Public Records, for the sole purpose of fatiguing them into compliance with his measures.

He has dissolved Representative Houses repeatedly, for opposing with manly firmness his invasions on the rights of the people.

He has refused for a long time, after such dissolutions, to cause others to be elected, whereby the Legislative Powers, incapable of Annihilation, have returned to the People at large for their exercise; the

State remaining in the meantime exposed to all the dangers of invasion from without, and convulsions within.

He has endeavoured to prevent the population of these States; for that purpose obstructing the Laws for Naturalization of Foreigners; refusing to pass others to encourage their migrations hither, and raising the conditions of new Appropriations of Lands.

He has obstructed the Administration of Justice by refusing his Assent to Laws for establishing Judiciary Powers.

He has made Judges dependent on his Will alone for the tenure of their offices, and the amount and payment of their salaries.

He has erected a multitude of New Offices, and sent hither swarms of Officers to harass our people and eat out their substance.

He has kept among us, in times of peace, Standing Armies without the Consent of our legislatures.

He has affected to render the Military independent of and superior to the Civil Power.

He has combined with others to subject us to a jurisdiction foreign to our constitution, and unacknowledged by our laws; giving his Assent to their Acts of pretended Legislation:

For quartering large bodies of armed troops among us:

For protecting them, by a mock Trial from punishment for any Murders which they should commit on the Inhabitants of these States:

For cutting off our Trade with all parts of the world:

For imposing Taxes on us without our Consent:

For depriving us in many cases, of the benefit of Trial by Jury:

For transporting us beyond Seas to be tried for pretended offences:

For abolishing the free System of English Laws in a neighbouring Province, establishing therein an Arbitrary government, and enlarging its Boundaries so as to render it at once an example and fit instrument for introducing the same absolute rule into these Colonies

For taking away our Charters, abolishing our most valuable Laws and altering fundamentally the Forms of our Governments:

For suspending our own Legislatures, and declaring themselves invested with power to legislate for us in all cases whatsoever.

He has abdicated Government here, by declaring us out of his Protection and waging War against us.

He has plundered our seas, ravaged our coasts, burnt our towns, and destroyed the lives of our people.

He is at this time transporting large Armies of foreign Mercenaries to compleat the works of death, desolation, and tyranny, already begun with circumstances of Cruelty & Perfidy scarcely paralleled in the most barbarous ages, and totally unworthy the Head of a civilized nation.

He has constrained our fellow Citizens taken Captive on the high Seas to bear Arms against their Country, to become the executioners of their friends and Brethren, or to fall themselves by their Hands.

He has excited domestic insurrections amongst us, and has endeavoured to bring on the inhabitants of our frontiers, the merciless Indian Savages whose known rule of warfare, is an undistinguished destruction of all ages, sexes and conditions.

In every stage of these Oppressions We have Petitioned for Redress in the most humble terms: Our repeated Petitions have been answered only by repeated injury. A Prince, whose character is thus marked by every act which may define a Tyrant, is unfit to be the ruler of a free people.

Nor have We been wanting in attentions to our British brethren. We have warned them from time to time of attempts by their legislature to extend an unwarrantable jurisdiction over us. We have reminded them of the circumstances of our emigration and settlement here. We have appealed to their native justice and magnanimity, and we have conjured them by the ties of our common kindred to disavow these usurpations, which would inevitably interrupt our connections and correspondence. They too have been deaf to the voice of justice and of consanguinity. We must, therefore, acquiesce in the necessity, which denounces our Separation, and hold them, as we hold the rest of mankind, Enemies in War, in Peace Friends.

We, therefore, the Representatives of the United States of America, in General Congress, Assembled, appealing to the Supreme Judge of the world for the rectitude of our intentions, do, in the Name, and by Authority of the good People of these Colonies, solemnly publish and declare, That these united Colonies are, and of Right ought to be Free and Independent States, that they are Absolved from all Allegiance to the British Crown, and that all political connection between them and the State of Great Britain, is and ought to be totally dissolved; and that as Free and Independent States, they have full Power to levy War, conclude Peace, contract Alliances, establish Commerce, and to do all other Acts and Things which Independent States may of right do. — And for the support of this Declaration, with a firm reliance on the protection of Divine Providence, we mutually pledge to each other our Lives, our Fortunes, and our sacred Honor.

Signed:

New Hampshire:

Josiah Bartlett, William Whipple, Matthew Thornton

Massachusetts:

John Hancock, Samuel Adams, John Adams, Robert Treat Paine, Elbridge Gerry

Rhode Island:

Stephen Hopkins, William Ellery

Connecticut:

Roger Sherman, Samuel Huntington, William Williams, Oliver Wolcott

New York:

William Floyd, Philip Livingston, Francis Lewis, Lewis Morris

New Jersey:

Richard Stockton, John Witherspoon, Francis Hopkinson, John Hart, Abraham Clark

Pennsylvania:

Robert Morris, Benjamin Rush, Benjamin Franklin, John Morton, George Clymer, James Smith, George Taylor, James Wilson, George Ross

Delaware:

Caesar Rodney, George Read, Thomas McKean

Maryland:

Samuel Chase, William Paca, Thomas Stone, Charles Carroll of Carrollton

Virginia:

George Wythe, Richard Henry Lee, Thomas Jefferson, Benjamin Harrison, Thomas Nelson, Jr., Francis Lightfoot Lee, Carter Braxton

North Carolina:

William Hooper, Joseph Hewes, John Penn

South Carolina:

Edward Rutledge, Thomas Heyward, Jr., Thomas Lynch, Jr., Arthur Middleton

Georgia:

Button Gwinnett, Lyman Hall, George Walton

DECLARATION OF INDEPENDENCE

CONSTITUTION OF THE UNITED STATES

We the People of the United States, in order to form a more perfect union, establish justice, insure domestic tranquility, provide for the common defense, promote the general welfare, and secure the blessings of liberty to ourselves and our posterity, do ordain and establish this Constitution for the United States of America.

Article I

Section 1. All legislative powers herein granted shall be vested in a Congress of the United States, which shall consist of a Senate and House of Representatives.

Section 2. The House of Representatives shall

be composed of members chosen every second year by the people of the several states, and the electors in each state shall have the qualifications requisite for electors of the most numerous branch of the state legislature.

No person shall be a Representative who shall not have attained to the age of twenty five years, and been seven years a citizen of the United States, and who shall not, when elected, be an inhabitant of that state in which he shall be chosen.

Representatives and direct taxes shall be apportioned among the several states which may be included within this union, according to their respective numbers, which shall be determined by adding to the whole number of free persons, including those bound to service for a term of years, and excluding Indians not taxed, three fifths of all other Persons.

The actual Enumeration shall be made within three years after the first meeting of the Congress of the United States, and within every subsequent term of ten years, in such manner as they shall by law direct. The number of Representatives shall not exceed one for every thirty thousand, but each state shall have at least one Representative; and until such enumeration shall be made, the state of New Hampshire shall be entitled to chuse three, Massachusetts eight, Rhode Island and Providence Plantations one, Connecticut five, New York six, New Jersey four, Pennsylvania eight, Delaware one, Maryland six, Virginia ten, North Carolina five, South Carolina five, and Georgia three.

When vacancies happen in the Representation from any state, the executive authority thereof shall issue writs of election to fill such vacancies.

The House of Representatives shall choose their speaker and other officers; and shall have the sole power of impeachment.

Section 3. The Senate of the United States shall be composed of two Senators from each state, chosen by the legislature thereof, for six years; and each Senator shall have one vote.

Immediately after they shall be assembled in consequence of the first election, they shall be divided as equally as may be into three classes. The seats of the Senators of the first class shall be vacated at the expiration of the second year, of the second class at the expiration of the fourth year, and the third class at the expiration of the sixth year, so that one third may be chosen every second year; and if vacancies happen by resignation, or otherwise, during the recess of the legislature of any state, the executive thereof may make temporary appointments until the next meeting of the legislature, which shall then fill such vacancies.

No person shall be a Senator who shall not have attained to the age of thirty years, and been nine years a citizen of the United States and who shall not, when elected, be an inhabitant of that state for which he shall be chosen.

The Vice President of the United States shall be President of the Senate, but shall have no vote, unless they be equally divided.

The Senate shall choose their other officers, and also a President pro tempore, in the absence of the Vice President, or when he shall exercise the office of President of the United States.

The Senate shall have the sole power to try all impeachments. When sitting for that purpose, they shall be on oath or affirmation. When the President of the United States is tried, the Chief Justice shall preside: And no person shall be convicted without the concurrence of two thirds of the members present.

Judgment in cases of impeachment shall not extend further than to removal from office, and disqualification to hold and enjoy any office of honor, trust or profit under the United States: but the party convicted shall nevertheless be liable and subject to indictment, trial, judgment and punishment, according to law.

Section 4. The times, places and manner of holding elections for Senators and Representatives, shall be prescribed in each state by the legislature thereof; but the Congress may at any time by law make or alter such regulations, except as to the places of choosing Senators.

The Congress shall assemble at least once in every year, and such meeting shall be on the first Monday in December unless they shall by law appoint a different day.

Section 5. Each House shall be the judge of the elections, returns and qualifications of its own members, and a majority of each shall constitute a quorum to do business; but a smaller number may adjourn from day to day, and may be authorized to compel the attendance of absent members, in such manner, and under such penalties as each House may provide.

Each House may determine the rules of its proceedings, punish its members for disorderly behavior, and, with the concurrence of two thirds, expel a member.

Each House shall keep a journal of its proceedings, and from time to time publish the same, excepting such parts as may in their judgment require secrecy; and the yeas and nays of the members of either House on any question shall, at the desire of one fifth of those present, be entered on the journal.

Neither House, during the session of Congress, shall, without the consent of the other, adjourn for more than three days, nor to any other place than that in which the two Houses shall be sitting.

Section 6. The Senators and Representatives shall receive a compensation for their services, to be ascertained by law, and paid out of the treasury of the United States. They shall in all cases, except treason, felony and breach of the peace, be privileged from arrest during their attendance at the session of their respective Houses, and in going to and returning from the same; and for any speech or debate in either House, they shall not be questioned in any other place.

No Senator or Representative shall, during the time for which he was elected, be appointed to any civil office under the authority of the United States, which shall have been created, or the emoluments whereof shall have been increased during such time: and no person holding any office under the United

States, shall be a member of either House during his continuance in office.

Section 7. All bills for raising revenue shall originate in the House of Representatives; but the Senate may propose or concur with amendments as on other Bills.

Every bill which shall have passed the House of Representatives and the Senate, shall, before it become a law, be presented to the President of the United States; if he approve he shall sign it, but if not he shall return it, with his objections to that House in which it shall have originated, who shall enter the objections at large on their journal, and proceed to reconsider it. If after such reconsideration two thirds of that House shall agree to pass the bill, it shall be sent, together with the objections, to the other House, by which it shall likewise be reconsidered, and if approved by two thirds of that House, it shall become a law. But in all such cases the votes of both Houses shall be determined by yeas and nays, and the names of the persons voting for and against the bill shall be entered on the journal of each House respectively. If any bill shall not be returned by the President within ten days (Sundays excepted) after it shall have been presented to him, the same shall be a law, in like manner as if he had signed it, unless the

Congress by their adjournment prevent its return, in which case it shall not be a law.

Every order, resolution, or vote to which the concurrence of the Senate and House of Representatives may be necessary (except on a question of adjournment) shall be presented to the President of the United States; and before the same shall take effect, shall be approved by him, or being disapproved by him, shall be repassed by two thirds of the Senate and House of Representatives, according to the rules and limitations prescribed in the case of a bill.

Section 8. The Congress shall have power to lay and collect taxes, duties, imposts and excises, to pay the debts and provide for the common defense and general welfare of the United States; but all duties, imposts and excises shall be uniform throughout the United States;

To borrow money on the credit of the United States;

To regulate commerce with foreign nations, and among the several states, and with the Indian tribes;

To establish a uniform rule of naturalization, and uniform laws on the subject of bankruptcies throughout the United States;

To coin money, regulate the value thereof, and of

foreign coin, and fix the standard of weights and measures;

To provide for the punishment of counterfeiting the securities and current coin of the United States;

To establish post offices and post roads;

To promote the progress of science and useful arts, by securing for limited times to authors and inventors the exclusive right to their respective writings and discoveries;

To constitute tribunals inferior to the Supreme Court;

To define and punish piracies and felonies committed on the high seas, and offenses against the law of nations;

To declare war, grant letters of marque and reprisal, and make rules concerning captures on land and water;

To raise and support armies, but no appropriation of money to that use shall be for a longer term than two years;

To provide and maintain a navy;

To make rules for the government and regulation of the land and naval forces;

To provide for calling forth the militia to execute the laws of the union, suppress insurrections and repel invasions;

To provide for organizing, arming, and disciplining, the militia, and for governing such part of them as may be employed in the service of the United States, reserving to the states respectively, the appointment of the officers, and the authority of training the militia according to the discipline prescribed by Congress;

To exercise exclusive legislation in all cases whatsoever, over such District (not exceeding ten miles square) as may, by cession of particular states, and the acceptance of Congress, become the seat of the government of the United States, and to exercise like authority over all places purchased by the consent of the legislature of the state in which the same shall be, for the erection of forts, magazines, arsenals, dockyards, and other needful buildings; — And

To make all laws which shall be necessary and proper for carrying into execution the foregoing powers, and all other powers vested by this Constitution in the government of the United States, or in any department or officer thereof.

Section 9. The migration or importation of such persons as any of the states now existing shall think proper to admit, shall not be prohibited by the Congress prior to the year one thousand eight hundred and eight, but a tax or duty may be imposed on such importation, not exceeding ten dollars for each person.

The privilege of the writ of habeas corpus shall not be suspended, unless when in cases of rebellion or invasion the public safety may require it.

No bill of attainder or ex post facto Law shall be passed.

No capitation, or other direct, tax shall be laid, unless in proportion to the census or enumeration herein before directed to be taken.

No tax or duty shall be laid on articles exported from any state.

No preference shall be given by any regulation of commerce or revenue to the ports of one state over those of another: nor shall vessels bound to, or from, one state, be obliged to enter, clear or pay duties in another.

No money shall be drawn from the treasury, but in consequence of appropriations made by law; and a regular statement and account of receipts and expenditures of all public money shall be published from time to time.

No title of nobility shall be granted by the United States: and no person holding any office of profit or trust under them, shall, without the consent of the Congress, accept of any present, emolument, office, or title, of any kind whatever, from any king, prince, or foreign state.

Section 10. No state shall enter into any treaty, alliance, or confederation; grant letters of marque and reprisal; coin money; emit bills of credit; make anything but gold and silver coin a tender in payment of debts; pass any bill of attainder, ex post facto law, or law impairing the obligation of contracts, or grant any title of nobility.

No state shall, without the consent of the Congress, lay any imposts or duties on imports or exports, except what may be absolutely necessary for executing it's inspection laws: and the net produce of all duties and imposts, laid by any state on imports or exports, shall be for the use of the treasury of the United States; and all such laws shall be subject to the revision and control of the Congress.

No state shall, without the consent of Congress, lay any duty of tonnage, keep troops, or ships of war in time of peace, enter into any agreement or compact with another state, or with a foreign power, or engage in war, unless actually invaded, or in such imminent danger as will not admit of delay.

CONSTITUTION OF THE UNITED STATES

Article II

Section 1. The executive power shall be vested in a President of the United States of America. He shall hold his office during the term of four years and, together with the Vice President, chosen for the same term, be elected, as follows:

Each state shall appoint, in such manner as the Legislature thereof may direct, a number of electors, equal to the whole number of Senators and Representatives to which the State may be entitled in the Congress: but no Senator or Representative, or person holding an office of trust or profit under the United States, shall be appointed an elector.

The electors shall meet in their respective states, and vote by ballot for two persons, of whom one at least shall not be an inhabitant of the same state with themselves. And they shall make a list of all the persons voted for, and of the number of votes for each; which list they shall sign and certify, and transmit sealed to the seat of the government of the United States, directed to the President of the Senate. The President of the Senate shall, in the presence of the Senate and House of Representatives, open all the certificates, and the votes shall then be counted. The person having the greatest number of votes shall be the President, if such number be a majority of the whole number of electors appointed; and if there be more than one who have such majority, and have an equal number of votes, then the House of Representatives shall immediately choose by ballot one of them for President; and if no person have a majority, then from the five highest on the list the said House shall in like manner choose the President. But in choosing the President, the votes shall be taken by States, the representation from each state having one vote; A quorum for this purpose shall consist of a member or members from two thirds of the states, and a majority of all the states shall be necessary to a choice. In every case, after the choice of the President, the person having the greatest number of votes of the electors shall be the Vice President. But if there should remain two or more who have equal votes, the Senate shall choose from them by ballot the Vice President.

The Congress may determine the time of choosing the electors, and the day on which they shall give their votes; which day shall be the same throughout the United States.

No person except a natural born citizen, or a citizen of the United States, at the time of the adoption of this Constitution, shall be eligible to the office of President; neither shall any person be eligible to that office who shall not have attained to the age of thirty five years, and been fourteen Years a resident within the United States.

In case of the removal of the President from office, or of his death, resignation, or inability to discharge the powers and duties of the said office, the same shall devolve on the Vice President, and the Congress may by law provide for the case of removal, death, resignation or inability, both of the President and Vice President, declaring what officer shall then act as President, and such officer shall act accordingly, until the disability be removed, or a President shall be elected.

The President shall, at stated times, receive for his services, a compensation, which shall neither be increased nor diminished during the period for which he shall have been elected, and he shall not receive within that period any other emolument from the United States, or any of them.

Before he enter on the execution of his office, he shall take the following oath or affirmation: — "I do solemnly swear (or affirm) that I will faithfully execute the office of President of the United States, and will to the best of my ability, preserve, protect and defend the Constitution of the United States."

Section 2. The President shall be commander in chief of the Army and Navy of the United States, and of the militia of the several states, when called into the actual service of the United States; he may require the opinion, in writing, of the principal officer in each of the executive departments, upon any subject relating to the duties of their respective offices, and he shall have power to grant reprieves and pardons for offenses against the United States, except in cases of impeachment.

He shall have power, by and with the advice and consent of the Senate, to make treaties, provided two thirds of the Senators present concur; and he shall nominate, and by and with the advice and consent of the Senate, shall appoint ambassadors, other public ministers and consuls, judges of the Supreme Court, and all other officers of the United States, whose appointments are not herein otherwise provided for, and which shall be established by law: but the Congress may by law vest the appointment of such inferior officers, as they think proper, in the President alone, in the courts of law, or in the heads of departments.

The President shall have power to fill up all

vacancies that may happen during the recess of the Senate, by granting commissions which shall expire at the end of their next session.

Section 3. He shall from time to time give to the Congress information of the state of the union, and recommend to their consideration such measures as he shall judge necessary and expedient; he may, on extraordinary occasions, convene both Houses, or either of them, and in case of disagreement between them, with respect to the time of adjournment, he may adjourn them to such time as he shall think proper; he shall receive ambassadors and other public ministers; he shall take care that the laws be faithfully executed, and shall commission all the officers of the United States.

Section 4. The President, Vice President and all civil officers of the United States, shall be removed from office on impeachment for, and conviction of, treason, bribery, or other high crimes and misdemeanors.

Article III

Section 1. The judicial power of the United States, shall be vested in one Supreme Court, and in such inferior courts as the Congress may from time to time ordain and establish. The judges, both of the supreme and inferior courts, shall hold their offices during good behaviour, and shall, at stated times, receive for their services, a compensation, which shall not be diminished during their continuance in office.

Section 2. The judicial power shall extend to all cases, in law and equity, arising under this Constitution, the laws of the United States, and treaties made, or which shall be made, under their authority; — to all cases affecting ambassadors, other public ministers and consuls; — to all cases of admiralty and maritime jurisdiction; — to controversies to which the United States shall be a party; — to controversies between two or more states; — between a state and citizens of another state; — between citizens of different states; — between citizens of the same state claiming lands under grants of different states, and between a state, or the citizens thereof, and foreign states, citizens or subjects.

In all cases affecting ambassadors, other public ministers and consuls, and those in which a state shall be party, the Supreme Court shall have original jurisdiction. In all the other cases before mentioned, the Supreme Court shall have appellate jurisdiction, both as to law and fact, with such exceptions, and under such regulations as the Congress shall make.

The trial of all crimes, except in cases of impeachment, shall be by jury; and such trial shall be held in the state where the said crimes shall have been committed; but when not committed within any state, the trial shall be at such place or places as the Congress may by law have directed.

Section 3. Treason against the United States, shall consist only in levying war against them, or in adhering to their enemies, giving them aid and comfort. No person shall be convicted of treason unless on the testimony of two witnesses to the same overt act, or on confession in open court.

The Congress shall have power to declare the punishment of treason, but no attainder of treason shall work corruption of blood, or forfeiture except during the life of the person attainted.

Article IV

Section 1. Full faith and credit shall be given in each state to the public acts, records, and judicial proceedings of every other state. And the Congress may by general laws prescribe the manner in which such acts, records, and proceedings shall be proved, and the effect thereof.

Section 2. The citizens of each state shall be entitled to all privileges and immunities of citizens in the several states.

A person charged in any state with treason, felony, or other crime, who shall flee from justice, and be found in another state, shall on demand of the executive authority of the state from which he fled, be delivered up, to be removed to the state having jurisdiction of the crime.

No person held to service or labor in one state, under the laws thereof, escaping into another, shall, in consequence of any law or regulation therein, be discharged from such service or labor, but shall be delivered up on claim of the party to whom such service or labor may be due.

Section 3. New states may be admitted by the Congress into this union; but no new states shall be formed or erected within the jurisdiction of any other state; nor any state be formed by the junction of two or more states, or parts of states, without the consent of the legislatures of the states concerned as well as of the Congress.

The Congress shall have power to dispose of and make all needful rules and regulations respecting the territory or other property belonging to the United States; and nothing in this Constitution shall be so construed as to prejudice any claims of the United States, or of any particular state.

Section 4. The United States shall guarantee to every state in this union a republican form of government, and shall protect each of them against invasion; and on application of the legislature, or of the executive (when the legislature cannot be convened) against domestic violence.

Article V

The Congress, whenever two thirds of both houses shall deem it necessary, shall propose amendments to this Constitution, or, on the application of the legislatures of two thirds of the several states, shall call a convention for proposing amendments, which, in either case, shall be valid to all intents and purposes, as part of this Constitution, when ratified by the legislatures of three fourths of the several states, or by conventions in three fourths thereof, as the one or the other mode of ratification may be proposed by the Congress; provided that no amendment which may be made prior to the year one thousand eight hundred and eight shall in any manner affect the first and fourth clauses in the ninth section of the first article; and that no state, without its consent, shall be deprived of its equal suffrage in the Senate.

Article VI

All debts contracted and engagements entered into, before the adoption of this Constitution, shall be as valid against the United States under this Constitution, as under the Confederation.

This Constitution, and the laws of the United States which shall be made in pursuance thereof; and all treaties made, or which shall be made, under the authority of the United States, shall be the supreme law of the land; and the judges in every state shall be bound thereby, anything in the Constitution or laws of any State to the contrary notwithstanding.

The Senators and Representatives before mentioned, and the members of the several state legislatures, and all executive and judicial officers, both of the United States and of the several states, shall be bound by oath or affirmation, to support this

Constitution; but no religious test shall ever be required as a qualification to any office or public trust under the United States.

Article VII

The ratification of the conventions of nine states, shall be sufficient for the establishment of this Constitution between the states so ratifying the same.

Done in convention by the unanimous consent of the states present the seventeenth day of September in the year of our Lord one thousand seven hundred and eighty seven and of the independence of the United States of America the twelfth.

CONSTITUTION OF THE UNITED STATES

BILL OF RIGHTS AND AMENDMENTS

Original Ten Amendments: The Bill of Rights, Passed by Congress September 25, 1789. Ratified December 15, 1791.

Amendment I

Freedoms, Petitions, Assembly

Congress shall make no law respecting an establishment of religion, or prohibiting the free exercise thereof; or abridging the freedom of speech, or of the press, or the right of the people peaceably to assemble, and to petition the Government for a redress of grievances.

Amendment II

Right to bear arms

A well regulated Militia, being necessary to the security of a free State, the right of the people to keep and bear Arms, shall not be infringed.

Amendment III

Quartering of soldiers

No Soldier shall, in time of peace be quartered in any house, without the consent of the Owner, nor in time of war, but in a manner to be prescribed by law.

Amendment IV

Search and arrest

The right of the people to be secure in their persons, houses, papers, and effects, against unreasonable searches and seizures, shall not be violated, and no Warrants shall issue, but upon probable cause, supported by Oath or affirmation, and particularly describing the place to be searched, and the persons or things to be seized.

Amendment V

Rights in criminal cases

No person shall be held to answer for a capital, or otherwise infamous crime, unless on a presentment or indictment of a Grand Jury, except in cases arising in the land or naval forces, or in the Militia, when in actual service in time of War or public danger; nor shall any person be subject for the same offence to be twice put in jeopardy of life or limb, nor shall be compelled in any criminal case to be a witness against himself, nor be deprived of life, liberty, or property, without due process of law; nor shall private property be taken for public use, without just compensation.

Amendment VI

Right to a fair trial

In all criminal prosecutions, the accused shall enjoy the right to a speedy and public trial, by an impartial jury of the State and district wherein the crime shall have been committed; which district shall have been previously ascertained by law, and to be informed of the nature and cause of the accusation; to be confronted with the witnesses against him; to have compulsory process for obtaining witnesses in his favor, and to have the assistance of counsel for his defence.

Amendment VII

Rights in civil cases

In Suits at common law, where the value in controversy shall exceed twenty dollars, the right of trial by jury shall be preserved, and no fact tried by a jury shall be otherwise re-examined in any Court of the United States, than according to the rules of the common law.

Amendment VIII

Bail, fines, punishment

Excessive bail shall not be required, nor excessive fines imposed, nor cruel and unusual punishments inflicted.

Amendment IX

Rights retained by the People

The enumeration in the Constitution of certain rights shall not be construed to deny or disparage others retained by the people.

Amendment X

States' rights

The powers not delegated to the United States by the Constitution, nor prohibited by it to the States, are reserved to the States respectively, or to the people.

Amendment 11

Lawsuits against states

The Judicial power of the United States shall not be construed to extend to any suit in law or equity, commenced or prosecuted against one of the United States by Citizens of another State, or by Citizens or Subjects of any Foreign State.

February 7, 1795.

Amendment 12

Presidential elections

The Electors shall meet in their respective states, and vote by ballot for President and Vice-President, one of whom, at least, shall not be an inhabitant of the same state with themselves; they shall name in their ballots the person voted for as President, and in distinct ballots the person voted for as Vice-President, and they shall make distinct lists of all persons voted for as President, and of all persons voted for as Vice-President, and of the number of votes for each, which lists they shall sign and certify, and transmit sealed to the seat of the government of the United States, directed to the President of the Senate;--The President of the Senate shall, in the presence of the Senate and House of Representatives, open all the certificates and the votes shall then be counted;--The person having the greatest number of votes for President, shall be the President, if such number be a majority of the whole number of Electors appointed; and if no person have such majority, then from the persons having the highest numbers not exceeding three on the list of those voted for as President, the House of Representatives shall choose immediately, by ballot, the President. But in choosing the President, the votes shall be taken by states, the representation from each state having one vote; a quorum for this purpose shall consist of a member or members from two-thirds of the states, and a majority of all the states shall be necessary to a choice. [And if the House of Representatives shall not choose a President whenever the right of choice shall devolve upon them, before the fourth day of March next following, then the Vice-President shall act as President, as in the case of the death or other constitutional disability of the President.]* The person having the greatest number of votes as Vice-President, shall be the Vice-President, if such number be a majority of the whole number of Electors appointed, and if no person have a majority, then from the two highest numbers on the list, the Senate shall choose the Vice-President; a quorum for the purpose shall consist of two-thirds of the whole number of Senators, and a majority of the whole number shall be necessary to a choice. But no person constitutionally ineligible to the office of President shall be eligible to that of Vice-President of the United States.

June 15, 1804.

Superseded by Section 3 of the Twentieth Amendment.

Amendment 13

Abolition of slavery

Section 1. Neither slavery nor involuntary servitude, except as a punishment for crime whereof the party shall have been duly convicted, shall exist within the United States, or any place subject to their jurisdiction.

Section 2. Congress shall have power to enforce these articles by appropriate legislation.

December 6, 1865.

Amendment 14

Civil rights

Section 1. All persons born or naturalized in the United States and subject to the jurisdiction thereof, are citizens of the United States and of the State wherein they reside. No State shall make or enforce any law which shall abridge the privileges or immunities of citizens of the United States; nor shall any State deprive any person of life, liberty, or property, without due process of law; nor deny to any person within its jurisdiction the equal protection of the laws.

Section 2. Representatives shall be apportioned among the several States according to their respective numbers, counting the whole number of persons in each State, excluding Indians not taxed. But when the right to vote at any election for the choice of electors for President and Vice President of the United States, Representatives in Congress, the Executive and Judicial officers of a State, or the members of the Legislature thereof, is denied to any of the male inhabitants of such State, being twenty-one years of age, and citizens of the United States, or in any way abridged, except for participation in rebellion, or other crime, the basis of representation therein shall be reduced in the proportion which the number of such male citizens shall bear to the whole number of male citizens twenty-one years of age in such State.

Section 3. No person shall be a Senator or Representative in Congress, or elector of President and Vice President, or hold any office, civil or military, under the United States, or under any State, who, having previously taken an oath, as a member of Congress, or as an officer of the United States, or as a member of any State legislature, or as an executive or judicial officer of any State, to support the Constitution of the United States, shall have engaged in insurrection or rebellion against the same, or given aid or comfort to the enemies thereof. But

Congress may by a vote of two-thirds of each House, remove such disability.

Section 4. The validity of the public debt of the United States, authorized by law, including debts incurred for payment of pensions and bounties for services in suppressing insurrection or rebellion, shall not be questioned. But neither the United States nor any State shall assume or pay any debt or obligation incurred in aid of insurrection or rebellion against the United States, or any claim for the loss or emancipation of any slave; but all such debts, obligations and claims shall be held illegal and void.

Section 5. The Congress shall have power to enforce, by appropriate legislation, the provisions of this article.

July 9, 1868.

Amendment 15

Black suffrage

Section 1. The right of citizens of the United States to vote shall not be denied or abridged by the United States or by any State on account of race, color, or previous condition of servitude.

Section 2. The Congress shall have power to enforce this article by appropriate legislation.

February 3, 1870.

Amendment 16

Income taxes

The Congress shall have power to lay and collect taxes on incomes, from whatever source derived, without apportionment among the several States, and without regard to any census or enumeration.

February 3, 1913.

Amendment 17

Senatorial elections

The Senate of the United States shall be composed of two senators from each State, elected by the people thereof, for six years; and each Senator shall have one vote. The electors in each State shall have the qualifications requisite for electors of the most numerous branch of the State legislature.

When vacancies happen in the representation of any State in the Senate, the executive authority of such State shall issue writs of election to fill such vacancies: Provided, That the legislature of any State may empower the executive thereof to make temporary appointments until the people fill the vacancies by election as the legislature may direct.

This amendment shall not be so construed as to affect the election or term of any Senator chosen before it becomes valid as part of the Constitution.

April 8, 1913.

Amendment 18

Prohibition of liquor

Section 1. After one year from the ratification of this article, the manufacture, sale, or transportation of intoxicating liquors within, the importation thereof into, or the exportation thereof from the United States and all territory subject to the jurisdiction thereof for beverage purposes is hereby prohibited.

Section 2. The Congress and the several States shall have concurrent power to enforce this article by appropriate legislation.

Section 3. This article shall be inoperative unless it shall have been ratified as an amendment to the Constitution by the legislatures of the several States, as provided in the Constitution, within seven years from the date of the submission hereof to the States by the Congress.

January 16, 1919. Repealed by the Twenty-First, December 5, 1933.

Amendment 19

Women's suffrage

The right of citizens of the United States to vote shall not be denied or abridged by the United States or by any States on account of sex.

Congress shall have power to enforce this article by appropriate legislation.

August 18, 1920.

Amendment 20

Terms of office

Section 1. The terms of the President and Vice President shall end at noon the 20th day of January, and the terms of Senators and Representatives at noon on the 3d day of January, of the years in which such terms would have ended if this article had not been ratified; and the terms of their successors shall then begin.

Section 2. The Congress shall assemble at least once in every year, and such meeting shall begin at noon on the 3d day of January, unless they shall by law appoint a different day.

Section 3. If, at the time fixed for the beginning of the term of the President, the President elect shall have died, the Vice President elect shall become President. If a President shall not have been chosen before the time fixed for the beginning of his term, or if the President elect shall have failed to qualify, then the Vice President elect shall act as President until a President shall have qualified; and the Congress may by law provide for the case wherein neither a President elect nor a Vice President elect shall have qualified, declaring who shall then act as President, or the manner in which one who is to act shall be selected, and such person shall act accordingly until a President or Vice President shall have qualified.

Section 4. The Congress may by law provide for the case of the death of any of the persons from whom the House of Representatives may choose a President whenever the right of choice shall have devolved upon them, and for the case of the death of any of the persons from whom the Senate may choose a Vice President whenever the right of choice shall have devolved upon them.

Section 5. Sections 1 and 2 shall take effect on

the 15th day of October following the ratification of this article.

Section 6. This article shall be inoperative unless it shall have been ratified as an amendment to the Constitution by the legislatures of three-fourths of the several States within seven years from the date of its submission.

January 23, 1933.

Amendment 21

Repeal of Prohibition

Section 1. The eighteenth article of amendment to the Constitution of the United States is hereby repealed.

Section 2. The transportation or importation into any State, Territory, or possession of the United States for delivery or use therein of intoxicating liquors, in violation of the laws thereof, is hereby prohibited.

Section 3. The article shall be inoperative unless it shall have been ratified as an amendment to the Constitution by conventions in the several States, as provided in the Constitution, within seven years from the date of the submission hereof to the States by the Congress.

BILL OF RIGHTS AND AMENDMENTS

December 5, 1933.

Amendment 22

Term Limits for the Presidency

Section 1. No person shall be elected to the office of the President more than twice, and no person who has held the office of President, or acted as President, for more than two years of a term to which some other person was elected President shall be elected to the office of the President more than once. But this Article shall not apply to any person holding the office of President when this Article was proposed by the Congress, and shall not prevent any person who may be holding the office of President, or acting as President, during the term within which this Article becomes operative from holding the office of President or acting as President during the remainder of such term.

Section 2. This article shall be inoperative unless it shall have been ratified as an amendment to the Constitution by the legislatures of three-fourths of the several States within seven years from the date of its submission to the States by the Congress.

February 27, 1951.

BILL OF RIGHTS AND AMENDMENTS

Amendment 23

Washington, D.C., suffrage

Section 1. The District constituting the seat of government of the United States shall appoint in such manner as the Congress may direct:

A number of electors of President and Vice President equal to the whole number of Senators and Representatives in Congress to which the District would be entitled if it were a state, but in no event more than the least populous State; they shall be in addition to those appointed by the States, but they shall be considered, for the purposes of the election of President and Vice President, to be electors appointed by a State; and they shall meet in the District and perform such duties as provided by the twelfth article of amendment.

Section 2. The Congress shall have power to enforce this article by appropriate legislation.

March 29, 1961.

Amendment 24

Abolition of poll taxes

Section 1. The right of citizens of the United

States to vote in any primary or other election for President or Vice President, for electors for President or Vice President, or for Senator or Representative in Congress, shall not be denied or abridged by the United States or any State by reason of failure to pay any poll tax or other tax.

Section 2. The Congress shall have power to enforce this article by appropriate legislation.

January 23, 1964.

Amendment 25

Presidential succession

Section 1. In case of the removal of the President from office or of his death or resignation, the Vice President shall become President.

Section 2. Whenever there is a vacancy in the office of the Vice President, the President shall nominate a Vice President who shall take office upon confirmation by a majority vote of both Houses of Congress.

Section 3. Whenever the President transmits to the President pro tempore of the Senate and the Speaker of the House of Representatives his written declaration that he is unable to discharge the powers and duties of his office, and until he transmits to them a written declaration to the contrary, such powers and duties shall be discharged by the Vice President as Acting President.

Section 4. Whenever the Vice President and a majority of either the principal officers of the executive departments or of such other body as Congress may by law provide, transmit to the President pro tempore of the Senate and the Speaker of the House of Representatives their written declaration that the President is unable to discharge the powers and duties of his office, the Vice President shall immediately assume the powers and duties of the office as Acting President.

Thereafter, when the President transmits to the President pro tempore of the Senate and the Speaker of the House of Representatives his written declaration that no inability exists, he shall resume the powers and duties of his office unless the Vice President and a majority of either the principal officers of the executive department or of such other body as Congress may by law provide, transmit within four days to the President pro tempore of the Senate and the Speaker of the House of Representatives their written declaration that the President is unable to discharge the powers and duties of his office. Thereupon Congress shall decide the issue, assembling within forty-eight hours for that purpose if not in session. If the Congress, within twenty-one days after receipt of the latter written declaration, or, if Congress is not in session, within twenty-one days after Congress is required to assemble, determines by two-thirds vote of both Houses that the President is unable to discharge the powers and duties of his office, the Vice President shall continue to discharge the same as Acting President; otherwise, the President shall resume the powers and duties of his office.

February 10, 1967.

Amendment 26

18-year-old suffrage

Section 1. The right of citizens of the United States, who are eighteen years of age or older, to vote shall not be denied or abridged by the United States or by any State on account of age.

Section 2. The Congress shall have power to enforce this article by appropriate legislation.

June 30, 1971.

Amendment 27

Congressional pay raises

No law, varying the compensation for the services of the Senators and Representatives, shall take effect, until an election of Representatives shall have intervened. May 7, 1992.

OTHER WORKS BY AMAZON CHARTS TOP 25 AUTHOR BOBBY AKART

The California Dreamin' Duology
ARkStorm (a standalone, disaster thriller)
Fractured (a standalone, disaster thriller)

The Perfect Storm Series
Perfect Storm 1
Perfect Storm 2
Perfect Storm 3
Perfect Storm 4

Black Gold (a standalone, terrorism thriller)

The Nuclear Winter Series

First Strike
Armageddon
Whiteout
Devil Storm
Desolation

New Madrid (a standalone, disaster thriller)

Odessa (a Gunner Fox trilogy)
Odessa Reborn
Odessa Rising
Odessa Strikes

The Virus Hunters
Virus Hunters I
Virus Hunters II
Virus Hunters III

The Geostorm Series
The Shift
The Pulse
The Collapse
The Flood

The Tempest
The Pioneers

The Asteroid Series (A Gunner Fox trilogy)
Discovery
Diversion
Destruction

The Doomsday Series
Apocalypse
Haven
Anarchy
Minutemen
Civil War

The Yellowstone Series
Hellfire
Inferno
Fallout
Survival

The Lone Star Series
Axis of Evil
Beyond Borders

Lines in the Sand
Texas Strong
Fifth Column
Suicide Six

The Pandemic Series
Beginnings
The Innocents
Level 6
Quietus

The Blackout Series
36 Hours
Zero Hour
Turning Point
Shiloh Ranch
Hornet's Nest
Devil's Homecoming

The Boston Brahmin Series
The Loyal Nine
Cyber Attack
Martial Law
False Flag

The Mechanics
Choose Freedom
Patriot's Farewell (standalone novel)
Black Friday (standalone novel)
Seeds of Liberty (Companion Guide)

The Prepping for Tomorrow Series (non-fiction)
Cyber Warfare
EMP: Electromagnetic Pulse
Economic Collapse

www.ingramcontent.com/pod-product-compliance
Lightning Source LLC
LaVergne TN
LVHW041958060526
838200LV00019B/386/J